Praise for *Pitching to the Dream Team*

"Christopher Bollas' insights are essential reading for any professional with strategic policy responsibility. Authentic societal choice cannot bear the unawareness that so often avails human reasoning. The hard choices, ambiguities, and anxieties that accompany the human experience will be enlightened by the wealth and breadth of Christopher Bollas' lectures." —**Mats Karlsson**, *former World Bank Vice President of External Affairs and United Nations Affairs and former State Secretary and Chief Economist in the Swedish Foreign Ministry*

"For the leaders, consultants, and coaches who are constantly dealing with repeated dysfunctional team dynamics, burnout, and discontentment in the workplace, Bollas gives a sustainable way to apply the unconscious and systemic thinking to break through polarizations and disputes and to embrace people in all the beauty of their messiness for ways forward. In times where "faster, bigger, and more" are reflexive but empty trends, *Pitching to the Dream Team* reminds us to slow down, be more intentional, and search deeper within ourselves and each other for perspectives and possibilities to bring people together. Particularly pertinent for Asia where the collective is the foundational unit of the society." —**Enoch Li**, Founder and Managing Director of Bearapy and Lecturer of Organizational Behaviour at INSEAD

"In a characteristically bold gesture that ventures beyond the classical Freudian paradigm of repression, Bollas addresses the systematic attack perpetrated by oppressive external forces on our capacity to think freely, creatively, and humanely. The central message of this book is that established organizational structures don't work. Imagine presenting an idea to a *dream team*, a work group with a genuine capacity for unconscious reverie and free association—and Bollas doesn't mean any old idea. The pitch concerns nothing less than finding a new way into a viable future. If, as Bollas maintains, the rim of chaos on our mental horizons is rapidly engulfing the present, then the creative act of seeing into the future involves a contemporary psycho-structural analysis of social catastrophes. Tasked by the logic of the present, *Pitching to the Dream Team* deftly maps the contours of our inner future."—**Steven Groarke**, Emeritus Professor of Social Thought at Roehampton University, London, and a member of the British Psychoanalytical Society

Pitching to the Dream Team

The INSEAD Lectures on Psychoanalysis and Organizational Life

Christopher Bollas

BLOOMSBURY ACADEMIC
NEW YORK • LONDON • OXFORD • NEW DELHI • SYDNEY

BLOOMSBURY ACADEMIC
Bloomsbury Publishing Inc, 1359 Broadway, New York, NY 10018, USA
Bloomsbury Publishing Plc, 50 Bedford Square, London, WC1B 3DP, UK
Bloomsbury Publishing Ireland, 29 Earlsfort Terrace, Dublin 2, D02 AY28, Ireland

First published in the United States of America 2026

Cover design: Enterline Design Services
Cover image © Christopher Bollas

A catalog record for this book is available from the Library of Congress.

ISBN: HB: 979-8-216-20203-5
ePDF: 979-8-216-20204-2
eBook: 979-8-216-20205-9

Typeset by Deanta Global Publishing Services, Chennai, India

Contents

Foreword

This book is composed of lectures to graduate students, faculty, alumni, and guests at INSEAD (Singapore) in September 2016. The task was to discuss the challenge to organizations posed by the pace and interlocking realities of globalization and to consider new ways of approaching the world of institutional relations (private sector, public, etc.) from a psychological perspective.

It may help to keep in mind that the chapters are transcribed talks, and in the interest of accuracy, there have been no changes to the original lectures other than to correct grammatical errors and eliminate redundant sentences.

Although some of the talks were written in advance, others were constructed on-site between the meetings, inevitably in response to the questions or comments of those attending.

What were we talking about?

We began with a question.

What could psychoanalysis bring to our consciousness as a tool for understanding, mitigating, and resolving conflict between groups and nations?

We discussed a new model—the dream team—aimed at increasing individual and collective creativity. In the background was the disturbing realization that Western organizations (top-down "creativity") that aimed to promote mental processes essential to dealing with the psychological complexities of organizational life in the twenty-first century were woefully inadequate.

The premise of the lectures was that all communities need to upgrade their understanding of human psychology in order to realize a latent maturity that is desperately needed in these times.

The group of some eighty people was mostly employed by NGO's and/or in private practice as independent consultants.

Consultative work with any organization—an institution, a company, or government—benefits from expertise in "group relations." Those psychoanalysts steeped in the work of Wilfred Bion, Elliot Jacques, and Pierre Turquet (amongst others) learned how Freudian analysis of the individual could work with a new form of group analysis.

The genius of Freud's "talking cure" was not limited to analytical sessions but could be employed in group relations tasked with sorting out conflicts on occasion between dire opponents. Indeed, it was quite astonishing to see how *over time* enemies could find themselves in each other (existential empathy) and speech both expressed and dissipated primitive and destructive states of mind.

The therapeutic irony—that to speak one's hate in the presence of the hated other is to dissipate it—was not lost on the participants, who could see with their own eyes that this worked.

The lectures focused on the view that traditional "top-down" or vertical structures of government and organization are inadequate to perceive, process, organize, and communicate the complexity of issues derived from the pace of information and events endemic to technological and cultural changes in the twenty-first century.

One of the alternatives to that form of information gathering, leadership, and organization was the democratic process of free association in which all participants' thoughts were voiced.

The Freudian vision—of a world free to speak its mind in the interests of a deeper understanding of our other self (our unconscious)—has enormous possibilities for application outside the clinical consulting room.

Although innovation will lead to artificial forms of intelligence that will have consequences for the human community, the human brain and our unconscious mental life have, all along, been uniquely suited to forms of perception, organization, and vision that are more than adequate to deal with the psycho-social challenges of market forces and other global realities.

The challenge is to develop those skills.

Our text begins with a published essay, "Psychoanalysis in the age of bewilderment," which was precirculated and the basis for our opening discussion. Readers will also find a short description of the topics under discussion for the first weekend, and the remainder of the book presents the lectures to follow.

In the twentieth century, psychoanalysis and the dynamic psychologies changed the way we viewed conflict. By considering states of mind—individual or collective—as important obstacles to resolving conflicts among groups in all sectors, we began the laborious process of including psychological means of conflict resolution.

From hostage negotiation to geopolitical mediation, we found ways to talk to a dangerous person or group, and through this talking cure, we significantly reduced the prospect of a turn to violence.

All along, however, certain praxes that had long preceded psychoanalysis were forerunners of the sort of mentality needed to put violent affects and primitive responses to the side in order that we use "higher-level functions" such as reason, empathy, and fidelity to the law.

Something as common as the debate team—where one had to empathize enough with often an odious position in order to win the contest—compelled us to frequently inhabit the mind of someone whose views we did not share. This *existential empathy* would inform the practice of law around the world, and even if the lawyers knew nothing about psychological clinical practice, they were practicing it.

We could list other contributions to the pool of knowledge that constitutes applied contemporary psychology, and these lectures hopefully join that movement.

We keep in mind that Homo sapiens, although distinct for higher-level mental and social organization than the other species, are capable of undergoing what we might term *acute phylogenetic regression*. Such regression is a natural outcome of abandoning our more civilized traits, leaving us to be as primitive as our primate cousins in the jungle. Such regressions are, unfortunately, pleasurable, and we must now face this truth: that when regressed many enjoy torturing, killing, raping, and hoarding.

Freud believed there were two core drives: the life and the death instincts. The life instinct is the self's engagement with new objects that inevitably enrich the self. The death instinct is a retreat from engagements, drawing back into the self, ultimately to death.

We can propose that there is another instinct, one that begins with the first Homo sapiens. This is the killer instinct that takes pleasure in raping, harming, or killing an innocent other. Freudians might argue that this is nothing more than an alignment of the sexual and aggressive drives, and indeed, it would emerge from them, but the killer instinct seeks to rape or murder. It evokes—draws upon—sexual and aggressive drives but also elicits a malignant narcissistic jouissance, which helps explain the euphoric state that such killers and rapists exhibit.

Readers unfamiliar with some of the neologisms I employ may want to refer to an excellent book by Sarah Nettleton titled on *The Metapsychology of Christopher Bollas* (2017).

Preface

Over the course of forty-five years working at the intersection of psychoanalysis, leadership psychology, and change management, we have witnessed a profound shift in how the human dimensions of organizational life are perceived and addressed. In our roles as Professors and Program Directors of the INSEAD Executive Master in Change (EMC) program, we have been helping executives integrate deeper self-awareness into their leadership practices. The program itself (founded in 2000–1 together with Manfred Kets de Vries and Gilles Amado) has underscored one inescapable truth: genuine leadership and organizational transformation require moving beyond superficial "quick fixes" to confront the unconscious and interrelated factors that shape individual, group, and organizational behavior. In doing so, EMC has adopted a systems-psychodynamic approach.

The book you are about to read resonates strongly with this perspective. Drawing on psychoanalytic insight, organizational dynamics, and a nuanced understanding of human change, it echoes many of the guiding principles that we embrace and teach at INSEAD. Through our background and training in psychoanalysis, we have long recognized the power of introspection—especially in fast-moving environments where leaders too often overlook the emotional and relational complexities underlying their individual and collective behavior and decisions. Bollas' dedication to free association, reverie, reflection, and creativity aligns perfectly with what is emphasized in the EMC as well as in other executive education programs: that sustainable leadership success stems from bridging head and heart, intellect and emotion, fantasy and reality, as well as logical and associative thinking.

The first part of this book provides an analysis of how the spaces and capacities to think fully and freely as leaders are eroding and under attack. Next to unconscious, inner-repressive psychodynamic forces (as outlined by Freud and others), Bollas identifies oppressive external systemic forces that attack and undermine the human capacity to think freely. Consequently, this opposes tapping into the rich, at times disruptive, as well as creative potential of the unconscious. Pitching to the *DreamTeam* provides a practical and detailed methodology that leaders can learn to develop this crucial capacity. Bollas proposes that creative and well-functioning organizations and societies require the capacity for collective, creative thinking and acting. This is also very much aligned with the mission of INSEAD, one of the world's leading business schools, which is to bring together people, cultures. and ideas in order to develop responsible leaders who transform business and society.

In our interactions with senior executives worldwide—from Europe, Asia, Africa, to the Americas—we have observed that leaders crave meaning and impact, whether in the boardroom or at home. Yet they seldom realize how vital it is to explore the unconscious: their fears, hopes, and desires that drive behavior. This book maps out precisely why such exploration is indispensable. By shedding light on unconscious processes—whether expressed in organizational practices, daydreaming, or cross-cultural interactions—it guides us to navigate the modern world with empathy, humility, and transformative vision. In so doing, this book offers a roadmap for leaders seeking not only higher performance but also a richer, more humane way of engaging with, within, and across families, organizations, and societies.

We invite you, as you read, to remain curious about what it evokes in you. Notice where you feel intrigued, confused, resistant, or inspired. Much like the participants in our EMC program, you may discover that what challenges you the most often holds the key to your greatest insight, understanding, and personal and professional growth. Our hope is that this book, in the terminology of Bollas, functions as a "shared object of thought." We hope it deepens individual and collective reflections about who we are—both as a leader and as a person. Bollas encourages us to embrace the full complexity and potential of the human psyche, as this might be one of the most significant factors promoting human, organizational, and societal progression.

Roger D. Lehman
Prof. Roger Lehman, Emeritus Senior Affiliate Professor of Entrepreneurship and Family Enterprise
INSEAD
roger.lehman@insead.edu
Prof. Dr. Erik L. H. M. van de Loo

Acknowledgments

I am very grateful to the three psychoanalysts who taught at INSEAD in Singapore and Fontainebleau and who arranged for my visit. I thank Roger Lehmann and Erik Van der Loos for conducting the seminar and organizing the visit, and my thanks to the program's eminent founder, Manfred Ket de Vries. I am also grateful to Jonathan Joyce, Meghan Kimani, Dustin Watson, and Lynn Zelem at Bloomsbury for their invaluable support with the text.

I owe a special debt to the late Gordon Lawrence, with whom I shared what I was learning from leading groups on unconscious thinking, and he brought his work on social dreaming to our meetings.

The Tavistock Clinic in the 1970s housed so many analysts and analytically oriented group relations staff—all basically sharing the same predicates—that it is more accurate to say that all of us training there shared the same basic assumptions. From Wilfred Bion to Elliott Jacques, from Sandy Bourne to Pierre Turquet, from Robert Gosling to Alexis Brook, the Tavi was guided by highly gifted people.

At the very same institution, Michael and Enid Balint, along with Peter Hildebrand, developed a group relations approach to consultancy with local GPs. Tavi trainees would be assigned to a surgery and develop a remarkable rapport with the GPs and their patients, a development that is thoroughly explored by Jonathan Sklar in his fine book *Balint Matters: Psychosomatics and the Art of Assessment*.

The Tavistock Institute of Human Relations was that wing of the organization solely dedicated to the study and "treatment" of organizations. This was the part of the Tavi that trained Gordon Lawrence and countless others who traveled the world teaching clinicians and organizational consultants how to identify, understand, and develop the psychology of groups. I thank Richard Jones for his intellectual acumen and guidance.

In the United States, I attended meetings of the Group for Applied Psychoanalysis (University of Buffalo), which was an eclectic gathering of people from many differing fields, and I found Warren Bennis' contributions on organizational dynamics inspiring. It was from Bennis that I learned of Talcott Parsons and others at Harvard who were "into" T-group theory and praxis.

A figure in the background of psychoanalysis is Sandor Ferenczi, whose interest in phylogenesis, group behavior, and culture was handed on to Geza Roheim, the greatest psychoanalytically informed anthropologist. It was at UC Berkeley in the 1960s that I had the good fortune to study with *the* expert on Roheim: the late Alan Dundes.

Finally, my obligation to my adolescent self and learning obliges me to acknowledge the work of Erich Fromm, whose writings changed my life. No writer in psychoanalytic history has integrated analytical thinking into the threads of other perspectives as brilliantly as he.

Abbreviations

FP	future pool of ideas
ICR	intersecting contextual realities
LOTP	logic of the present
POK	pool of knowledge
RWG	reverie work group
SOOT	shared object of thought
DC	dynamic consciousness

The Lectures

Introduction

Each era in world history has compelled human groups or civilizations to face the uncertainty of the future. Although the monotheisms (and other religions) provide compelling narratives that ordain a future, our secular self must nonetheless use its wits to find a way into a viable future.

By the nineteenth century, novelists were writing science fiction to imagine the future, and now the twenty-first century is predicated on constant and fast-moving inventions of the future, accelerated by IT technology, the internet, and the structure referred to as "globalization."

Stephen Hawking and many credible visionaries predict that AI will result in mass unemployment in the near future. Set against this vision is its opposite; indeed, in the Hegelian sense, it's antithesis. Rather than a world expanding outwards with increasingly complex non-human connections, there is evidence of an opposition to globalization, one that may create real-time crises for organizations of all stripes around the world.

In these sessions, however, the focus will be on changes in human personality that are at the least an indirect result of the IT age. We might term them new "ego forms": i.e., new ways of human adaptation to the globalized world. We will consider new patterns in thinking, in behaving—that are adaptive—and we will consider unconscious factors in human personality that are intentionally or not sabotaging what the world has taken to be progress.

Participants are encouraged before our afternoon meetings to "flesh out" those parts of their organizational lives that pair with the morning's discussion. In particular, the "modular" paradigm that has governed our social organizations (a CEO, a board, shareholders, or a prime minister, Parliament, an electorate, etc.), although reflecting social patterns that have existed for thousands of years (c.f. religious organizational hierarchies), is to some extent redundant. Traditional concepts of leadership based on vertical structures of authority and governance, while necessary up to a point, are obsolete in light of the speed, magnitude, and horizontal implications of actions in the world.

It will be argued that unconscious processes (of perception, organization, formulation, and action planning) must be utilized by organizations in order to keep pace with events that are themselves concordant with the speed—indeed the nature—of unconscious events. What do we think of this?

Specific terms will be given to types of personality change that have been evoked by the twenty-first century, as well as social and national shifts that need objectification and thinking.

While the morning sessions focus on laying out the challenges posed by the imminent unknown—a future that is all too soon upon us rather than in some distant temporal locality—the afternoon sessions will turn to "problem-solving" the challenge posed. What *forms* of organization might we turn to in order to meet the specific *formal challenge* of globalization and the IT world?

Given the strains on group and individual characters posed by the twenty-first century, what can organizations do to alleviate the predictable human suffering of living in a high-stress world that might sack one at the drop of a hat?

What new *political forms* might be generated that are adaptive to the challenges of globalization? And how do we conceptualize and generate a new sense of meaning in a world where millions of people, although technologically enfranchised, are feeling an inner emptiness that at present is unaddressed?

We begin with a precirculated essay.

1 Psychoanalysis in the Age of Bewilderment

On the Return of the Oppressed

"I came into the world imbued with the will to find a meaning in things, my spirit filled with the desire to attain to the source of the world, and then I found that I was an object in the midst of other objects. . . . Sealed into that crushing objecthood, I turned beseechingly to others."[1] —Frantz Fanon

"Our own period is constitutionally one of desperation. What I say is that it is a period of disorientation, nothing more."[2] —Jose Ortega y Gasset

It is perhaps fitting that this conference takes place here in the "City Upon the Hill." The Puritan elders of the early seventeenth century not only sought refuge from European religious persecutions, but believed that in founding a New Israel would "cast a light" upon a Europe living in sin. They set impossibly high standards for themselves and their children and within the first generation were shocked by their own crimes. In *Of Plymouth Plantation*[3] Governor Bradford (who arrived on the *Mayflower*) confronted the aftermath of a disturbing trial in which the plaintiff—Thomas Granger—was tried for serial bestiality. At his trial, various animals were brought into the room, and he had to identify those with whom he had committed these "foul" acts.

Granger was found guilty and executed in September 1642. "A very sad spectacle it was" writes Bradford because "for first the mare and then the cow and the rest of the lesser cattle were killed before his face, according to the law, Leviticus xx.15; and then he himself was executed." The animals were buried in a large pit.

Bradford tries to understand why men of faith could commit such an act. He momentarily considers that perhaps "profane people" had mixed in with the migrants, but he dismisses this and turns to a psychological explanation.

Another reason may be that it may be, in this case, as it is with waters when their streams are stopped or dammed up. When they get passage they flow with more violence and make more noise and disturbance than when they are suffered to run quietly in their own channels; so wickedness being here more stopped by strict laws (352) so that they are forbidden to "run in a common road of liberty" and search for an outlet "where and at last breaks out where it gets vent." (352)

The Puritan mentality—the idealized self aiming to save the world through the display of an exemplary being—generated axioms that over time would contribute to the American grain: a country and its citizens devoted to their own innocence, insistent they were the land of the free and the home of the brave destined to lead the world into the future. The eminent American historian, Richard Hofstadter, described this mentality in *The Paranoid Style in American Politics*.[4]

Bradford was shaken by the immediate outbreak of aberrant behavior amongst his fellow Puritans. Several hundred years later Freud's vision of humanity is shattered by the Great War. Writing to Lou Andreas-Salomé in November 1914:[5] "I know for certain that for me and my contemporaries the world will never again be a happy place. It is too hideous . . . humanity seems to be really dead."[6] (21) Five months later, he is writing the first draft of *Thoughts for the Times on War and Death*.[7] He begins his essay with a caveat: He is too close to the war to take his personal views as objective. Then he writes:

> *Standing too close to the great changes that have already taken place or are beginning to, and without a glimmering of the future that is being shaped, we ourselves are at a loss as to the significance of the impressions which press upon us and as to the value of the judgements which we form. (275)*

Freud's remarkable essay could be read as a commentary not only on the War but on the stunning changes brought about by the Industrial Revolution. In just over 100 years lives around the world had been transformed. In his essay, Freud points to the progress made in the nineteenth century, but he is overwhelmed by the War and its implicit cancellation of all the Enlightenment assumptions he held so dear. He writes that the non-combatant is "a cog in the gigantic machine of war—[who] feels bewildered in his orientation, and inhibited in his powers and activities." He seeks consolation by focusing on two themes—disillusionment and death—but he concedes that he is seeking some understanding to gain perspective: "I believe that he [his reader] will welcome any indication, however slight, which will make it easier for him to find his bearings within himself at least." (275)

The "cog in the gigantic machine" would do as a metaphor for the tens of thousands of factory workers who made up the working class. If Dickens, facing the impact of the Industrial Revolution, could still write "It is the Best of Times, It is the Worst of Times" and find something redeeming in the good sides of humanity, by the time of the Great War it would be harder to hold onto the positive aspects of social progress.

Scientific advances would prove to be the one salient exception, leading almost all secularists to embrace this new form of hope.[8]

Otherwise, only by splitting off from consciousness the mind-boggling forces of human destructiveness (passive or active)[9] could people in the early twentieth century retain belief in progress as the fabric of the world community was being torn to shreds.

We note.

In the last thirty-five years of the nineteenth century, 80 percent of Africa was invaded and colonized by the European powers, many getting a slice of what King Leopold of Belgium called "this magnificent African cake" (viii).[10] If *Goethe's Faust* (1808) can be read as an uncanny manifesto of the greed and callousness about to unleash itself on humanity in the name of industry and progress, then Conrad's *Heart of Darkness* (1899) seems to offer an end of century accounting for the profound oppression unleashed by armed greed. Colonialism was many things, but perhaps above all it was the march of absolute ignorance invading rather than understanding the human universe. Kurtz's dying words, "the horror, the horror," are both an epitaph to the nineteenth century and an uncanny foretelling of the twentieth century to follow.

In his *Autobiography,* Yeats observes the "growing murderousness of the world."[11] Pondering the Great War in 1919, in perhaps the most visionary poem ever composed ("The Second Coming"), he writes:

> *The blood-dimmed tide is loosed and everywhere*
> *the ceremony of innocence is drowned.*

Between Conrad and Yeats—in the twenty years separating the passages above—we see the drowning of innocence—in blood.[12]

When Freud writes that his fellow kind do not even have "a glimmering of the future" he also registers the shock of his times but he also identifies an emerging psychic loss. How can we envision a future if the recent past and the present *defer* human vision?

To think about the future is to form a crucial mental structure that gathers unconscious visions ("bearings") of possible futures and orients the self in the temporal existentiality of the life span. To think about the future is to exercise an important mental function vital to[13] the survival of the self and the species.

Frantz Fanon: "The structure of the present is grounded in temporality. Every human problem cries out to be considered on the basis of time, the ideal being that the present always serves to build the future. . . . The future must be a construction supported by man in the present. This future edifice is linked to the present insofar as I consider the present something to be overtaken." (xvi–xvii)[14]

These days, we may notice a deepening pessimism about the future. Indeed, even discussing it seems to miss the point of contemporary life as we appear to gradually slip away from negotiating our realities and accept a selective perception of the world that is turning negative hallucination into an art form.[15] We may seek refuge and consolation in the nourishing aspects of life—falling in love, the pleasures of relationship, the meaning of raising a family, the creativity of work—but could this human resilience now be a hindrance to survival? By taking refuge in the present are we abandoning the future?

Freud concentrated on the censorship that leads to the repressed unconscious. Derivatives of the repressed would show up in sessions through the versatile veils of language that could disguise highly complicated buried fantasies or memories from censorial consciousness.

At the same time—indeed from the century before—another form of censorship gathered mass and structure. This was a censorship organized not against unacceptable sexual or aggressive contents, but against the self's right *to be*. Oppression came in countless forms and histories—the lives in the working class, the oppression of women and children, the domination of countries by terrifying dictators, those leaders who sent millions to their deaths, the "cumulative trauma"[16] of war after war after war after war, the assimilation of human beings into the system capitalism such that its "forces" override the rights of man.

Freud's censor, ironically enough, generated a remarkably intelligent response from the fecund creativity of the unconscious—indeed, to the point that some might argue it is the foundation of verbal freedom driven by the need to fulfill wishes—the oppressor inculcates in the oppressed a different set of reactions.

When studying the effects of slavery on the human subject,[17] the distinguished historian Kenneth Stampp argued that slaves feigned types of stupidity which actually constituted a form of resistance. Whether they "accidentally" broke machinery or appeared too ignorant to follow instructions, Stampp points out that slaves not only resisted, but committed actions that I think of as the *return of the oppressed*. Their "bungled actions" were not indications of the return of the repressed, but forms of resistance to oppression. We may think of this defense as pseudostupidity.[18]

Frantz Fanon wrote that he was "overdetermined from the outside"[19] and used Freud's concept of overdetermination to focus on the effect of the other's oppression of the self rather than one's own self-censorship. [20]

How do we identify oppression as a specific category for psychoanalysis? After all, life in itself is somewhat oppressive, and at various times we all feel oppressed. What do I mean *within the realm of psychoanalysis* by oppression and the return of the oppressed?

The repressed refers to the elimination from consciousness of specific mental contents. The oppressed refers to the suspension or distortion of human thinking. The repressed returns through the rerouting of ideas. The oppressed refers to an alteration not of the *contents* of the mind, but of the *capacities* of the mind—the way one forms thoughts. When discussing the course of oppression, we note a cumulative degradation of the *forms* of perception, thought, and communication.

If the repressed refers to the temporary elimination of an idea from consciousness, the oppressed refers to the compromise of the mental process that would have constructed the thought to begin with. The repressed resides in the system unconscious—indeed for Freud it defines the unconscious. The oppressed *is* to be found in the unconscious but as a *failed effort*, the trace of what might have been ideationally created (even if banished) and linking up to other forms of such failure.

The cumulative effect of thousands upon thousands of such failed possibilities forms a mental network of *the mangled*— of ideas half formed but left disabled. The history of this sad evolution leaves the self at a loss, in a state of unconscious grief, and a mourning that, if it goes unrecognized, can be endless.[21] In the extreme, a self de-formed would be left—if driven to express its contents—burdened further with the impossibility of translating the aggregate of contents into senseable ideas.

From the beginning aspects of the psychoanalytical method—the freedom to put ideas formed as the unthought known into speech—have mitigated the oppressions suffered by analysands. The *care* given to the speechless self, exemplified in the works of Ferenczi, Balint, Winnicott, Khan, Coltart, (and more recently in the works of Michael Parsons, Jonathan Sklar, and Roger Kennedy) implicitly recognizes the reality that some selves suffer "overdetermination from the outside." The pathway to cure—whether through mitigating the pain of distressing contents or through the forms offered for articulation of one's being—is the same in a Freudian analysis. Cure takes place through the transformations of both into sentient speech, contained and sustained by the attentive care of the deeply listening analyst.

When the oppressed are returned through psychoanalysis, it is *transformed* from compromised forms of reception, thought, and communication into the ordinary forms by which we live.

Aspects of the way we communicate and think in the twenty-first century can be seen as forms of *psychic flight* from the overwhelming burden of inheriting a world shattered by regions of dumb thoughtlessness resident in the preceding two centuries.

The internet allows psychically systemic[22] flight from the actual, as we live in a virtual reality with varied avatars of the self. We both are and are not deeply involved in communicating our views on the various issues of the day. Avatars allow us to speak through alternate personalities that permit engagement with one another online, but although Facebook seems to be an exemplar of the transparent self, even there, our points of view are more like photo snaps of our engagements in the actual world.

Danah Boyd[23] writes that teenagers' use of texting, etc., is not driven by wishes but by oppression. Anxious parents do not want their children playing on the streets of America (the author noted in her travels that, unlike in the twentieth century, contemporary children are not playing with one another). Instead, they set up countless activities for them so they rarely have a chance to socialize except by internet.

Perhaps, then, the development of a virtual self engaged in quick and shallow speech (tweeting allows only 140 characters per communication) is a compromise formation between transparency and absolute silence. Cryptic speech keeps people in touch with one another but not close. Little about the self is revealed, and little from the other is engaged.

What we have instead of the depth of communication are spectacles from the mental shallows.

Let us pause a moment to appreciate a significant difference between the individuals whom Freud saw and those we see in the twenty-first century. From the seventeenth through the late nineteenth century, the wanderer and then the flaneur provided a viewpoint of the self. (Rousseau famously proclaimed, "I must walk in order to think!") Viewing the object world—whether a river, a book on botanical monographs, and so forth—involved the self's immersion in a relatively unmediated real. This was the matrix of *le vecu* (or lived experience), and Freud's understanding was that the "psychic values" that generated dream thoughts were evoked by the self's private experience in the quotidian. What he cannily exploited for his technique was knowledge that unconscious life depends upon the self's engagement with evocative objects[24] and the wandering self—constantly moved by its unconscious engagements with the object world—was to prove a rich storehouse of recollections in the tranquility of the analytical consulting room. (Or the hysteric analysand *remembering* these vivid moments had a rich basis for mingling the imaginary and the actual transforming infirmity into an art form.)

The psychic values of the contemporary analysand will be based less on unmediated experiences and more on those indirect perceptions spawned by the information revolution. It is as if contemporary selves live several steps removed from engagements in the real—retreating from the unmediated due to anxieties about life outside its gated communities, seeking ironic sanctuary in the technology of mediation.

In another essay,[25] I discussed the new role of the self as a transmitter of information, via Twitter or Facebook. The Arab Spring exemplified how people *convey the news* and see themselves as vital to the act of transmission. iPhones and other such technical devices are *transmissive objects,* prosthetic parts of the contemporary self. The workers in the assembly lines of the nineteenth century were estranged from their positions, but the twenty-first-century self identifies himself as *part* of the machinery of communication, not simply a figure who assembles and works the object.

Few writers of the late twentieth and twenty-first centuries capture the spirit of our age as well as North American novelist Don DeLillo.

In *Cosmopolis,*[26] DeLillo writes: "The speed is the point. We are not witnessing the flow of information so much as pure spectacle, or information made sacred, ritually unreadable." (80)

In his brilliant, if disturbing work *Mindless: Why Smarter Machines are Making Dumber Humans*[27]Simon Head, senior fellow at the Institute for Public Knowledge at NYU and senior member of St. Anthony's College Oxford, traces and dissects the disseminative influence of "computer business systems" (CBSs) on workers in almost all aspects of the "managed" world: manufacturing, service industry, the financial world, and elsewhere. As CBSs program workers to speed up their work rate—through almost minute-by-minute instructions for working throughout the day, individual judgment is systematically replaced by manuals that tell people exactly how to behave and what to say.

"There is an unrelenting emphasis on the need for speed in the execution of processes," writes Head (25). "The human element" he argues "is completely absent in this perfecting of process" (26).

DeLillo: "People in free societies don't have to fear the pathology of the state. We create our own frenzy, our own mass convulsions, driven by thinking machines that we have no final authority over" (85).

So the twenty-first-century self is programmed into a Fastnet[28] world that mandates speed at the expense of reflection; indeed, of judgment itself. Part of Head's argument is that as processes become more efficient humans become "dumber" because human thought slows down the efficiency of systems. We can already see the effect of the CBS on psychoanalytical practice with calls for evidence-based manuals that will make psychoanalysts more efficient. Setting that ambition aside, the mentality generated by CBSs promises to the population quick, *readymade pre-existent* solutions.

The demand for quick-fix assurances has not snuck up on those people working in the world of "mental health." For decades, insurance companies, HMOs, national health services, and other "providers" have sought briefer forms of psychotherapy than the one delivered by psychoanalysis. To some extent, psychoanalysts have adjusted to this, but the trends toward the quick fix have sponsored an axiom that the issues of mental life (whether the form of a symptom, the dense thickets of moods, or the issues generated by one's personality) should be remedied by the consumption of a *product* that will *remove* troublesome issues.

Now there is a new axiom: the solution to the problem of mental life is to follow a program that provides action guidance. In contemporary society, there is a shift to supporting evidentially effective forms of treatment that *work*. What *message* can the patient take from the consulting room hour that will help him to improve his life? What comments by the analyst will prove to be *operationally* effective?

Insurance companies want to know, governments investing money in mental health want to know, and patients, caught up in the rush to solve problems, *expect* to know—and to know quickly.

In subtle ways, we may observe a shift in some of our patients, away from the merit of the unknowable productiveness of unconscious thinking toward the value of knowable remedies that can be put into effect immediately. This type of operational thinking seeks cognitive analogues to the ingestion of medication that will be immediately effective.

Upon hearing an interpretation, this sort of analysand will receive it less as part of a sequelae of conscious discontinuities connected by unconscious processes and more as a "stand free" or "stand alone" sound bite that might serve as a program for alteration of the self's behavior. How often are we hearing these days "Okay, I get it. So all I have to do now is to . . . ."[29]

One effect of operationalism[30] is the inclination to develop action statements over reflection.

A clinical sample.

"I notice that you seem to take what I say as an implicit set of instructions for how you can improve yourself" which might elicit [Patient:] "Isn't that the point of it?" While being sympathetic to that understanding one might reply "Well it might seem so, but by immediately putting it into a plan for behavior change, I wonder if you have actually given yourself time to think about it?"[31]

When this interpretation of the formal aspect of the analysis is understood, it is then possible to discuss ancillary dimensions: the analysand's feeling that he does not have time to give matters thought, the anxiety that he must come up with a solution to himself, the unconscious fantasy that the mind is a trouble-making entity that needs formulaic structuring in order to be updated by an android implant.

Focusing on what works might seem smart, but in this new utilitarianism we witness an emerging soft nihilism in which the human subject—and the complex processes of thought—are *implicitly* viewed as an impediment to the successful implementation of programs that may be person-dependent. In the internal world, unconscious conflicts and reflective thought are clearly too slow, and a hindrance in what proposes itself as problem-solving era but which, actually, is an age increasingly devoted to the trimming down of the human dimension.

If our species has always, in differing ways, doubted the validity of any prevailing worldview, there has nonetheless always been some form of vertical (or hierarchical) cosmology that makes one thing more important than another. Belief in one's God, for example, would have been put higher on the list of significance than, say, belief in what the weather would be the following week. Whether right or wrong in their beliefs or in their priorities, people for thousands of years have not had difficulty establishing vertical structures of thought. In the twenty-first century, however, we see a new form of thought emerging: horizontalism,[32] the eradication of prioritization of thought in favor of equivalencies that make all ideas equally valid.

A sample of horizontalism:

> *Imagine I say to a patient "You seem to cope with your envy of your friend by making yourself indispensable to him" and the reply is "Uh, oh, YEAH! And I also do too much bike riding and stuff like that. And now that you say this, I also do . . . yeah . . . way too much bike stuff." To which I might say "Are you thinking that enviously driven help and riding your bike are the same?"*

Horizontalism does not recognize any hierarchical order. All things are equal and no one thing is intrinsically more important than another. The Fastnet and transmissive selves do not necessarily register the weight of meaning of any object of communication. We may see this on cable news, for example, where a series of fires in the Western part of the United States, or an impending hurricane, will be given the same air time as a war in the Ukraine or a genocide in Africa. The recognized value of the opinions of highly experienced journalists, scholars, and writers now fades out as the social democracy of the internet turns everyone into an expert on any topic. While this democratization is hugely beneficial in many respects, the downside is the inadvertent promotion of the power of the uninformed self.

When vertical thinking is destroyed and horizontal thought prevails, then *difference* between one topic another another becomes meaningless. Indeed, differentiation is predicated on the ability to evaluate and to discriminate between objects; to find in alterity a tensional creativity as difference generates oppositions that will be valued if heterogeneity is assumed to be of value. But the process of globalization promotes a global-self, a uniform being that even if only ever a fiction (it could never become a reality) may nonetheless function as a psychic soporific for homogenized human beings. So, to operationalism and horizontalism we add homogenization: the need to eradicate difference and fashion a world of common beings. The promotion of homogeneity aims at the reduction of difference, the lessening of tensions, and the presumed increase in the productive potential of the human being.

In the psychoanalytical situation, homogenization takes the form of the analysand's fear of being perceived as different ("but doesn't everyone think what I just said?"). The Fastnet makes identification and fusion with others so easily accomplished that from day to day millions of people are "on the same page," often sharing the same spectacles, which promotes the sense that one is part of a collective norm (40 percent of the world's population now has internet access).

Which brings me to the difference between sight and insight. Many observers consider this an era of "the spectacle."[33] We seem drawn to the sights of life often found in the mediated universe. We may be sightfully informed (i.e., we have memories of what we have seen) but have comparatively little insight. Insight is not possible without consciousness being directed toward the internal world, or without interest in the psychodynamics of our own being.

This does not mean that contemporary selves are uninterested in what others see of them. Posting pictures of the selves ventures on Facebook asks for "feedback": "what do you see when you see me?"

The analysand may see into the self *through* the analyst's interpretation, but he then assumes that such indeed is the function of the analyst. Although the analyst does not intend to produce an intellectual commodity we might term "an insight"[34]the patient—whom I suppose now we could re name "the consumer"—purchases what is said.

"But I do remember what you said a few weeks ago" a patient might say demonstrating that what was taken to be an insight was no such thing at all. Instead it was "a sight into the self" created by the analyst's interpretation. It can be recollected by the patient, but has no lasting effect. We may be facing a new challenge to the heart of analysis: the self is becoming a spectacle in the universe of observable objects. Attention to analysis of the mind and its contents is news-in-itself, meritorious as a sight one presumably wishes to see.

Seeing may be believing, but is it knowing?

Let us call the phenomenon that uses sight in order to avoid insight *sightophilia*. A person who is unusually drawn to seeing (rather than thinking) is a sightophile.

A feature of sightophilia is *refractive* thinking. An object of refractive thought leads to instantaneous emissive ejection of a lie (or lines of thought) outward—away from the subject—into space. Refraction will cast thought onto objects, but they will not serve as containers for such thoughts (retrievable upon memory), only as surface conduits for the dispersal of the remnants of illumination until the content of a thought is eventually eliminated.

Refractive skill selects a minor feature of communication and highlights it, sending the core communication to oblivion.

I say to a patient, "I think you are being indispensable to your friend allows you to covertly attach yourself to her." He replies, "You got it. I am indispensable, and I should watch it if it becomes too much. That's brilliant, thanks so much." I say "You seem to have grasped this thought so quickly that I am not sure we have had a chance to think it, and, you also seem to have put it into action, just like that. What do you think?" "Oh, I just think it was great. Am I . . . am I . . . meant to think about it?"[35]

In the best of these times, then, the psychoanalyst may be morphed into a wise sage, appreciated in much the way one might be grateful for a good auto mechanic or computer expert. In place of insight, we have sight: albeit analytically informed sight. In place of reflective thought, we have refractive thinking or operational imperatives. In place of carefully constructed vertices of meaning specific to the psychic and lived history of a subject we have a homogenized being, dynamically amalgamated (and updated) by horizontal objects of thought.

"Because time is a corporate asset now" writes De Lillo "it belongs to the free market system. The present is harder to find. It is being sucked out of the world to make way for the future of uncontrolled markets and huge investment potential. The future becomes insistent." (79). Are the new dimensions of thinking I have explored forms of efficiency that now seem embedded in assumptions about being and relating? Or are we in a more indeterminate era, where these types of thought are intermediate adaptations to a changing world in which we are now thinking by not thinking?

We will keep this in mind as operationalism, horizontalism, homogenization, pseudostupidity, refraction, sightophilia, etc., may be transiently adaptive moves adopted to control the bewildering.

Following Badiou, Jameson,[36] and others, it seems a fair question to wonder if suspension of thought and engagement—a form of psychic retreat[37]—is dawning evidence of subjecticide. Less than fifteen years separate Heiddeger's question, "why is there being rather than nothingness?" and Camus', "why not suicide?" Subjecticide would eliminate any need for actual suicide, as one is now provided with many vehicles to eliminate the pain of being a subject.

(As I use the term, the "subject"[38] is the self's process of thought and expression.)

Subjecticide would be the self's elimination of the integrity of thought that supported the illusion of the "I." It's not its grammatical position that is eliminated—obviously people still use the first person—but what if being, relating, and existing as a "first person" feels too problematic? Not only because of the postmodernist critique that the subject was an illusion all along—making postmodernist thought perhaps the first final philosophical objectification of subjective suicide—but because the elimination of previous categories of existence (family life, citizenry, generation of meaning, etc.) has left selves without agency? What if, indeed, those of us who once felt this way are in a form of grief and mourning, while those for whom the subject was never known proceed as objects in the world of other objects?

I have termed this move—from being a subject to being an object—"objecthood"[39] to identify flight from the mind. One should, instead, be a good "communicator"—a transporter or transmitter of ideas that collect humanity into an integrated and unified form of being.

In earlier essays, I wondered if we were entering a period of normopathy in which the normopath or the normotic[40]—that person who aims to be an object in the world of other objects—is licensed to enter the world of the ordinary as long as individual idiosyncratic existence is ostensibly eliminated.

The psychoanalytical struggle to understand, objectify, and analyze character disorders remains an interest of most analytical groups today, but by the end of the twentieth century, there was an increased focus across the analytical world on the issue of "thinking." This preoccupation was perhaps associated with the profound impact of the work of Wilfred Bion, but one must also note the works of Harry Stack Sullivan, David Rapaport, Donald Meltzer, Ignazio Matte-Blanco, and André Green. There is emerging a new lexicon of terms devoted to the ability (or not) to think thoughts, and so with ADHD and the rise of cognitive behavioral psychology we seem to see a broader preoccupation with the problems of thinking.

Is the interesting work of Peter Fonagy and colleagues on "mentalization"[41] a register of the problem facing contemporary analysts with analysands who seem to lack the ability to think about themselves? The perils of such an assumption are obvious in that we might be on the verge of creating a world of the "haves" and the "have nots": that is those who can think about their internal worlds and those who cannot. But Fonagy's work speaks to thousands of psychoanalysts and although we must always entertain the possibility that the analytical movement is capable of a histrionic reaction to the arrival of seemingly new phenomena, I do believe that we are witness in the twenty-first century to different ways of thinking.

When Freud writes of disillusionment in *Thoughts for the Times on War and Death*, he does so having celebrated in this essay—in stunningly moving prose—the "new fatherland": a world view redolent with implicit ideals. But the War "tramples in blind fury all that comes in its way, as though there were to be no future" (279) and although he tries to recuperate himself by returning to his understanding of what later he would term the death drive, he still mourns the loss of illusions: "We welcome illusions because they spare us unpleasurable feelings, and enable us to enjoy satisfactions instead" (279). Throughout the nineteenth and twentieth centuries we have ample evidence that, even in the face of the traumatic effects of the Industrial Revolution, people managed to sustain illusions of the good life and to relate to an ordinary ideal self.

We may see the ideal self (and its projections into an ideal society or world) as an essential companion. That intrapsychic relationship was a rather crucial counterpoint to the dulling effects of the amoral world of modern capitalism.[42] From the Second World War to Iraq, from the Holocaust to the Rwanda genocide, the human passion for murder has, amongst other things, destroyed any possibility of the humanist ideal self. Freud's vision of man as equidistant between the life and death instincts is harder to sustain as the sheer magnitude and processional independence of the death instinct now outweighs the life instinct.[43]

We might think of the early twenty-first century as the Age of Bewilderment.

Scientific and technological changes continue—although I would argue at a less rapid pace than in the nineteenth or twentieth centuries—and intimate human relations and individual creativity survive in the harshest of times. But the widening socio-economic divide, the alarming deterioration of world climate,[44] the assimilation of international terrorism into multicultural societies, the failures of even the "advanced" parts of civilization to learn from the horrors of the past (cf the Ukraine as a possible repeat of the Crimean War), the degradation of the nation state and the emergence of a the new public realm of the globalized, have not so much given pause for thought as simply given pause. Is it the sheer *magnitude* of the problems besetting our world? We are not any more destructive than before, but we are *far* more dangerous. This has generated both fear and helplessness not seen on this scale before, especially given the *refractive* "thought" process of social media that does not internalize, contain, metabolize, and contextualize issues, but shimmers the spectacles of danger into billions of bizarre objects.

A secular world without ideals[45] or vertical meaning has left the populations of the twenty-first century living in an era where bewilderment is not simply an aftereffect of the previous two centuries but a defensive posture.[46] If we cannot construct good dreams for selves, families, regions, nations and the world; if we therefore cannot construct the future as a mental object collecting those dreams and utilizing them for vital matrices that connect citizens of all nations in a meaningful progression, then as adaptive creatures we have turned to new strategies in order to tread water.

"God is dead" may have been the iconic, melodramatic mantra of the late nineteenth century, but what if we are now facing a new mantra: "Mankind is dead"?

Yeats may have been right about some "rough beast, its hour come round at last, moving toward Bethlehem to be born." This is, perhaps, a foretelling of religious fundamentalism[47] in the monotheisms, but the atheistic parts of all selves may be balancing this fervour with an anodyne self that seems to lack all conviction.

The cluster of defensive forms identified in this essay obviously arises from the culture of the global community. They emerge from what Winnicott termed the "third area": the area of cultural experience. Unlike the classical psychiatric nomenclature, which identifies specific disorders deriving from individuals, third area transmissions are negotiated unconsciously by the large group that we have referred to as nations or now as the world. Winnicott's concept of the false self does not describe a specific disorder but a function of personality that will be more or less pronounced depending on the threat to the true self.

The concept of the false self becomes pertinent to human psychology when the subject is impinged upon by a disturbance from the real. The "average expectable" reality that Hartmann[48] wrote about in the seminal text *Ego Psychology and the Problem of Adaptation* is no longer average and certainly not expectable. In reaction to the instability of reality we see mentalities developing that protect the core self by constructing a type of false self that dulls the subject's recognition of reality: indeed, elects not to see it.[49]

The fundamentalist and anodyne self marry in the registers of sociopathy. The first is devoted to homicide, the second to suicide.

In conclusion, I have considered how contemporary global culture may be producing a collective mentality adaptive to the mind-boggling challenges posed by the rim of chaos on our mental horizons. While our societies continue to be creative in the sciences and in technology—indeed to the point of their deification—and while the privileged take refuge in the aesthetics of materialism, our capacity for destruction endangers all species and the planet itself. Those disciplines noteworthy for thoughtfulness (including psychoanalysis) are of decreasing interest to even the most advanced societies.[50] And the world of mainstream cinema now mandates standardized action films because language-based movies are too costly to translate and hence to globalize. The economic spin-off of such homogenization is huge, as figures of the heroes (and their worlds) are sold around the world.

Is the shock of a world seemingly beyond human influence and comprehension verging on the unthinkable? Are we unconsciously identifying with the process of oppression, a form of identification with the aggressor, ironically aimed at the diminution of generative human capability? Are we in the grip of a collective death drive paralyzing us from affecting change?

A passage from J.-B. Pontalis:

> *the death instinct asserts itself in a radical* **unbinding process,** *a process of* **enclosure** *that has no aim but its own accomplishment and whose repetitive nature is the sign of its instinctivity. This is a process that no longer has anything to do with conscious death anxiety but which* **mimics death** *in the being's very nucleus. . . . Then the psyche is no longer a substitutive representative of the body. It* **is** *body. The unconscious can no longer be deciphered through its* **formations**, *in a mobile and articulable logic of "signifiers," it is realized and immobilized in the logic of the psychical body.*[51]

In those ego formations that constitute the return of the oppressed, do we mimic death?

The shot into the future by the Industrial Revolution generated profoundly creative and manic attempts[52] to catch and represent the meaning of human life before thinking fell by the wayside. The twentieth century may be viewed as the era when, across the intellectual spectrums of the West, the failure to formulate viable ideas about a meaningful life may have left a generation not only in mourning but in a somewhat disabling melancholia. If so, the generations of the twenty-first century inherit a world of the mentally compromised, although hope always resides in the remarkable resilience indigenous to being human.

2 Return of the Oppressed

We have considered how certain forms of thinking—increasingly evident in the twenty-first century—may be driven by the demands of the industrialized world for the more efficient self.

Physically tortured people walking free from their torturers will show in the way they walk and try to talk compromises in their way of being. Those who are oppressed over long periods of time may also show changes in the way they think, talk, and relate.

I referred to a *constellation* of mental *forms* that I propose are evidence of cumulative oppression, including: horizontalism, operationalism, homogenization, pseudostupidity, refraction, and sightophilia.

To repeat:

> *Horizontalism eradicates hierarchic thinking, rendering mental contents equal. No one idea has more merit than another.*

Homogenization eliminates differences and fuses diversity into the agglomerated. Efforts to distinguish ideas from one another are defeated.

Operationalism *converts* reflective thought into action schemas. It is a type of "action-thought" to quote Kohut, in which psychoanalytical interpretation is quickly formulated into a plan of action that discards any reflection.

Refraction also replaces reflection by refusing to receive the integrity of a thought, shattering it into pieces, dissolving its fragments into the stream of stripped ideas.

Sight replaces insight. Spectacles are sought as truths in themselves in a world that displaces language with images. Think of the urge to produce, transmit, and consume images, all accomplished with remarkable speed.

Pseudostupidity is an attempt to dumb down the self in order to fit in with the idiom of the era and to avoid thoughts that might trouble the self and its others.

These patterns of thought are not endogenous formations responsive to intrapsychic forces—instincts, affects, memories, and so forth—and they therefore lack the complex interlacing imbrication of a self's profoundly idiosyncratic psychodynamic. They are mentalities promoted in contemporary culture to which the ego will adapt.

(I use the term "ego" to refer to our unconscious structure and its evolving organization of the self and its mental life. It is composed in the first years of life, derived from innumerable operational assumptions communicated by the parental world through emotional, psychic, verbal, and physical handling of the self as infant and toddler. An unthought knowledge base is established early on that will radiate and disseminate its assumptions during the course of one's lifetime.)

Although this knowledge (the unthought known) is developed primarily within social psychology rather than driven from the depths of psychic life, it becomes part of one's being. The ego easily splits to accommodate the vagaries of, and divergences between, the many differing realities of an existence: endogenous, somatic, familial, communal, marital, vocational, national, and so forth.

Tens of thousands of axioms eventually become regular patterns that run the self, like the engine and machinery of an automobile, but we are now on the verge of a self overwhelmed by increasing regulatory demands imposed by the complexities of modern life.

Freud understood the early twentieth-century self as one crippled by psychoneurotic issues, derived from unacceptable wishes or thoughts. The superego—the part of the mind that judges all of our thoughts (conscious and unconscious)—ordained repression and the ego obliged by finding a compromise between total suppression of a wish and willy-nilly fulfillment of them.

But the price of civilization is that selves are now dominated less by a superego than by an ego that oppresses the self through deeply compromised forms of being.

The return of the repressed—a necessary focus for early twentieth-century psychoanalysis—refers to the return of unwanted mental *contents* through disguised articulation.

I am proposing a related idea: the return of the oppressed. This refers to the appearance of unwanted *forms* of thinking and representation that have been subjected to negative transformations when: reflective thought is replaced by refractive shimmering; linguistic articulation is transformed into "-K" cryptic sound bites; historical thinking is displaced by expedient confabulation.

(The letter "K" is used by psychoanalyst Wilfred Bion to refer to thoughts or communications that develop knowing or knowledge, while "-K" refers to mental actions aimed at ridding the self of knowledge.)

The return of unwanted ideas rewords content so that the idea, insofar as consciousness is concerned, is permissible in disguised articulation. The return of unwanted forms (of perception, thinking, and communicating) leads to dumbed-down thought structures that degrade the capacity to think.

Both types of return involve alteration of the banished.

Both involve complex defenses against mental pain.

Both aim to satisfy human wishes.

A self suffering considerable repression may reveal impoverishments of thought and affect, even if the drive to return the repressed leads to intriguing symptoms, dreams, linguistic formulations, or artistic creations. A self enduring cumulative oppression must establish forms of expression that, even in a minimalist sense, do express aspects of the self.

The return of the oppressed may be a form of mental suicide, or subjecticide. Subjecticide offers the self an ego position in the new social order through the elimination of sophisticated forms of perception and thoughtfulness.

Part of the challenge facing the present-day psychoanalyst is how to restore interest in being a subject. The theme of this congress is "tools" that the analyst can use to address modern issues. What tools can the analyst use to analyze oppression and the return of the oppressed? How and in what ways can psychoanalysis offer orientation and points of view during the Age of Bewilderment?

"Times winged chariot" compels me to choose only one clinical emphasis and, unfortunately, to exclude other vital tools we have at our disposal. Regrettably, I leave out how crucial it is to identify and interpret the formal changes to the ego—that is, to analyze mental structures of the oppressed.

So too I leave out the role of historical reconstruction in helping people to transform the mute facts of their past into a meaningful history crucial to the *contextualization* of selves many of whom now live outside of history: personal, familial, cultural, transnational. I also leave out the field of "inter-relating" which includes the transferences and the countertransferences, formed through the relational milieu cultivated by the two participants.

I shall instead focus on select aspects of free association, considered in terms of the twenty-first-century self as we concern ourselves with how we can enrich ourselves and our communities through liberated thought processes.

Freud, as we know, was a dialectical thinker who in his writing sustained many differing lines of thought—often in creative contradiction to one another—and his various views of the function and the method of free association reflected his intellectual idiom. He was more of the nineteenth than the twentieth century, the age in which Walt Whitman said of thinking: "Do I contradict myself? Very well, then, I contradict myself; I am large—I contain multitudes." And like Whitman, Freud's interlacing *multitudinous* lines of thought, crisscrossing one another in accord and then in discord—on the same topic—mime the very nature of unconscious processes of thought themselves. Like a poem, they are simply manifest evidence of unconscious thinking and creativity.

In order to reduce the mystique of the term "free association," I like to use a synonym—"free talking." This is what we wish the analysand to do: simply to talk—to move spontaneously between ideas and topics without attempting to organize them. This is because the discourse of the unconscious takes place not in the disclosure of any one single thought, but in the gaps between discontinuous units of discourse. It is when the analysand *changes topic* from "a" to "b"—that he or she unknowingly reveals a "chain of ideas" that *is* unconscious thought. In other words, unconscious meaning is revealed in the logic of sequence.

Some of the thought-forms of the twenty-first century—pseudostupidity, refraction, and horizontalism, and so on,—often manifest themselves through vague or abstract speech.

"I suppose I had a kind of ok time last weekend" or, "I had a row with my partner last night and so I am a bit bummed out today." Or, "Well, um, I didn't have a good time at the conference, just sort of drifted off, you know."

In these examples of comments by patients, we may see a -K abstraction that rids the self of contact with psychic reality through utilization of empty statements.

Before the analyst can contemplate exactly what generates these summaries, he needs to know *in detail* from what they are abstracted.

"You did not have a good time at the conference?" with an inflected interrogative usually elicits psychic material.

As the defensive obfuscation of abstraction is lifted and the details are provided, the analysand is *unknowingly* free associating. He may think he is just recollecting the events of the day but as his unconscious selects the logic of sequence he speaks the unconscious. To quote Virginia Woolf, he has entered the "poetry of existence."[1]

In time, as those "chains of ideas" become the evidence produced by psychoanalysis, both the analyst and the patient develop a "third ear" to listen to them. In this respect, as always but of even greater significance these days, free association creates new idioms of listening, intensifying and disseminating the self's ability to unconsciously comprehend the world.

As the analysand speaks the details and the analyst gathers from time to time the patterns of thought, the lengthy task of establishing a vital intrasubjective object relation between conscious self and unconscious being begins. This relation, unique to psychoanalysis, evolves slowly, developing what we might think of as dynamic consciousness—consciousness that appreciates, receives, and uses unconscious thinking with deliberate skill.

The psychic follow-on of this realization is profound, and its conceptualization is the self's full comprehension of what it *is* to be a subject. It is to be *there* as a conscious being continuously and endlessly *moved* by one's unconscious interests.

To speak is to discover the value of language. The end of the twentieth century has been characterized as witness to the death of language ("linguisticide") giving way to sign-systems: of emotiveness, shared platitudes, clichés, and so forth. To rediscover language in the era of the anodyne is to empower the subject as he turns toward the tasks of introspection.

To discover, or rediscover, the pleasure of language constitutes an important *emotional* experience. Articulation releases suffocated affects and emotions, buried or foreclosed both by the inability to speak and by the limits of enactment.

To describe the details of one's thoughts is to establish over months and then years what we may think of as *psychoanalytical day residue*. These daily reports and associations provide access to moments of "high psychic value" and then generate dreams that will arise only from being in an analysis.

Free association then may elicit curiosity. Where before there may have been little interest in the individual search for meaning, now the self is producing highly significant articulations from the analytical sessions, contributing to what Freud termed "the storehouse of ideas."

These days, we have something of an intriguing reversal of the twentieth-century use of free association. Whereas before, the self, meandering in the everyday, encountered objects in lived experience that gathered psychic momentum in order to be dreamed—a nodal junction for the dissemination of the meanings of that day—nowadays people retreat into the mentally denuded realms of the normopathic universe that insulates the self against significance in the lived. People still dream, but analytical effort *to link* the dream to the vivid events of the preceding day will often fail. Such salient moments have often not been registered by a self that is defended against receiving and allowing them to form vertices of meaning.

This means that sessions *create* the day residue through accounts of events in reality. Free talking generates emotional experiences and epiphanies in the hour that may then promote dream life afterward.

The dream, then, is the genera that emerges from such psychic immersions and is a new midpoint. (Psychic genera[2] are another type of après-coup: instead of congealing deferred pain they congregate deferred inspiration.) An inspired idea is a genera. It is the outcome (the aftereffect) of perhaps a long period of psychic work that gestates until unconscious thinking presents a lucid idea to consciousness.

Dreams—and free associations to them—now transfer mental significance *into* the following day's lived experiences, animating the object world with a vitality and meaning that have been missing.

Whereas the oppressed return, ordinarily, via the complex of mental forms I have outlined, through psychic genera psychoanalysis allows a transformation from increased freedom of speech to a freedom of thought. From there, one gains insight into the mentalities occupying the self.

The struggle to preserve contact with our internal world is, no doubt, phylogenetic. But in our era, so preoccupied with war and survival, there is little time for reflective thought. The normopath is not a new personality presence; indeed, few descriptions of this ego formation surpass E. M. Forster's depiction of it in *Howards End*.[3] Henry Wilcox, businessman, chortles, "I am not a fellow who bothers about my own inside" (119). "It was hard-going in the roads of Mr. Wilcox's soul" writes Forster as "he simply did not notice things, and there was no more to be said" (119). His thoughtful and rather long-suffering wife, Margaret, tries to confront him. It is one of the most famous passages in English literature:

> *Only connect! That was the whole of her sermon. Only connect the prose and the passion, and both will be exalted, and human love will be seen at its height. Live in fragments no longer. (119)*

Many critics citing this passage have wrongly concluded that "only connect" refers to human relationships: that we need to connect more with one another. In fact, Forster refers to connecting affect with language. In this respect, his theory is startlingly similar to Freud's first vision of the transference, where he argued that the transference was the connection of thought with language: the transfer of an emotion-idea into speech.[4]

In both Forster and Freud, we see a priority given to the matriculation of emotion into language, a passion that, of course, brings people together. I submit that the core features of psychoanalysis—especially the work of free association—connect feelings with words and in this way are incrementally transformational, especially in the early twenty-first century when we may be witness to a widespread diminishment of our capacities for thought and expression.

3 Organizational Pathologies and the Compound Syndrome

Changes in behavior and personality are not new, of course. If we were to track back to the late nineteenth century and to Kraft-Ebbing in *Psychopathia Sexualis,* we would find interesting sexual practices that were entirely contingent upon the use of handkerchiefs. It would seem that this piece of clothing, made popular by the vestimentary requirements of the nineteenth century generated intriguing perversions and certainly aided the female hysteric who often required remedy by handkerchief.

The essay you have read (Chapter 1) maintains that the wars and genocides of the twentieth century set Western societies into a prolonged period of mourning over the loss of modernist assumptions that had evolved from at least the mid-eighteenth century. The roots of the modern era go back as we know to fifth-century Greece; indeed, as far back as to Sumeria and 2,500 BCE. We may see the existentialist movement as a form of melancholia—that is mourning mixed in with anger—over this loss.

Indeed, it is interesting that it was in 1951 that Robert Knight of the Menninger Clinic named a new ego form—a new idiom of psychopathology—which he termed "the borderline personality." That personality is characterized by the lack of a core sense of self, displaced by a constant state of mental turmoil driven by passing affects. The borderline self is almost constantly enraged but initially tries to form highly idealized relations to others in what might be seen as an effort to create a safe and sound and good world only to have this smashed to pieces by even very slight disappointments.

This person, therefore, always lived on the border between an ideal world and a terrible one: with no intermediate space. It was an "Either/Or" frame of mind, and if we choose to see this disorder within history it certainly mirrors a world crisis: are we humanist saints or are we vile monsters? This term, "the borderline personality," was to become the predominant personality disorder of the mid- to late twentieth century.

The systematic detachments characteristic of the end of twentieth-century philosophy—what is popularly termed "post modernism"—may be seen as an effort to end this melancholia by claiming that any self, or society, or culture are merely illusions that at best testify to our need for one or another narrative to live by. If the borderline population had no core self, the postmodernists would seem to be arguing that it was an illusion to begin with and that we are simply occupants of varying mental positions passingly defined by whatever narrative we choose to describe our life to ourselves.

In the 1970s, I noted what I took to be a new form of personality emerging —what I termed the "normotic" or what Joyce McDougall terms "the normopathic." It was my view that normotics were characterized by families (and their children) seeking meaning through the acquisition of material objects and a life of recreational action—and other activities—in order to avoid the life of the mind.

The terms "normotic" or "normopath" may have been new, but many writers had written about what D. W. Winnicott termed "abnormal normality" a topic that engaged Erich Fromm's interest for a long time.

As mental life is challenging—brought on by ordinary stages of development and relationships—the normopathic solution emptied selves of a certain capacity for insight and depth of thought. Lecturers in the academic world were alarmed that more young people seemed startlingly lacking in both interest and experience in self-examination. Psychoanalysts, influenced especially by the work of Bion, turned to the question of thinking.

As discussed, one of his major contributions was to identify two forms of knowing, what he termed "K" (the search for knowledge) and "-K," the urge to eliminate knowledge or knowing the self. We may include in the intellectual history a notion that the turn toward Bion throughout the psychoanalytical world—especially in the 1990s—was evidence of a widespread recognition of a shift in the clinical population. People were less thoughtful and we needed to create a vocabulary to discuss this problem within the clinical community. As many of you know, Bion worked with groups and his theory of thinking became crucial to many who worked at the Tavistock Institute of Human Relations which applied psychoanalytical thinking to the study of organizations.

In the chapter, I noted that many modern selves are decreasingly interested in the inner world—of dreams, daydreams, inner imaginings, and so on—and more determined to be efficient. A single image may suffice as it is suggestive: that young people spend many hours each week jogging but the three hundred years tradition—inaugurated in our minds by Rosseau—of walking simply to see the surrounding world—a movement of mind, body, and spirit that generated food for thought (inspiring countless visions, whether we were poets or novelists, scientists, merchants or farmers) seems to have vanished from the epistemic tradition.

Instead, the jogging self—either on the streets or treadmill—often is encased in an ipad listening to music so that the sounds of the actual world are eliminated. The self is moving so quickly there is little time to take in the tapestry of the real, let alone to direct a gaze at single objects that may prove evocative, or to nod at people and "take them in."

Looking back at the essay, you will recall that I argue that the ego (the term Freud used to signify a self's unconscious organization) has always adapted to changing circumstances. Indeed, adaptation is one of the primary characteristics of ego intelligence, and an ego adapts by *changing itself* rather than altering reality.

We might state that any ego is, therefore, counter-political in that whatever the circumstances, our ego will alter itself in order to facilitate our survival.

This said, it is clear that if there are large-scale social changes, as we see now in the twenty-first century, then there will be new ego formations that adapt to those changes.

Again, I leave it to you to pick up any of the ego forms I discussed in the essay—such as horizontalization—but the main argument is that while before we employed machines (or technology) to assist us—and therefore were the masters of that universe—the concern expressed by many writers is that we are both unwittingly and unconsciously becoming a part of the machine itself.

That is, as the sheer pace and complexity of the new era demands decision making that is impossible for individual or even collective consciousness to grasp as before in situ, we have adapted to this alteration by *becoming part of the system itself.* To be more specific, we are not simply *identifying* with technology, we are intrinsic links in its functioning and we unconsciously see ourselves as such. Many of the objects we use in social media are what I term "transmissive objects" and the new generations have become "transmissive selves" passing on what they see to others through social media, identified and identifying with the act of transmission rather than the work of analysis.

We could spend time discussing Twitter, where we are altering not simply the way we spell, or construct sentences, but where we mime the encrypted speech of social media.

I now return to our focus on ego adaptations to reality.

Looking at how the ego is changing, we observe another idiom of change in social life, or what we term a "syndrome." The Merriam-Webster dictionary defines a syndrome as "a group of signs and symptoms that occur together and characterize a particular abnormality or condition." The word originates from the Greek combination of "sun" (together) and "dramein" (to run) to form the single word "sundrome." So, we hear in this word "together we run" an important comprehension of how syndromes can change personality if together we run in a particular way.

For all the envy directed at the 1 percent (billionaires), those of us in psychoanalysis who see some of these people in analysis are noting what I term the "Compound Syndrome." The topic is too large to discuss in full here, but it is characterized by a diminishment in the ego strength of its selves precisely because they have retreated into enclaves in which everything is provided for them.

It is observable in families where selves have multiple homes, private jets, an entourage of cooks, masseuses, fitness trainers, and yes . . . therapists, to the point where they are no longer personally engaged in commerce with the outside world. Without knowing it this withdrawal into the gated community is the work of the death drive. The outside world is regarded as unsafe (and it may be so), unreliable (no doubt), unseemly (surely so in parts), and any number of other "negatives." By withdrawing into enclaves these selves are unwittingly promoting a type of psychic anorexia in which there is a huge loss of "food for thought": that is, a diminishment in adventurous curiosity that is vital to the life instincts.

So the syndrome is "together we are running into carefully constructed enclaves where we believe we have everything."

In my profession, a task is to help these people leave the compound because the syndrome weakens the self both mentally and somatically. (I am sure an entire host of somatic symptoms—especially headaches and neurasthenia—are evolving from this trend in living.)

We all know that globalization cannot succeed if it is only for the 1 percent, even if we try to console ourselves by claiming that it has indeed benefited the poor in the world, which to some extent it has. But the increasing disparity not simply of wealth but of the objects that wealth supplies is unconsciously fomenting an opposition to the life instincts of globalization through the death drive. (Commerce involves selves in joining the lives of others while the Compound insulates selves).

To remind us, Freud did not pen his theory of the life instincts and the death instincts as moral criteria but as observations on two distinct—and necessary—forces in human nature. The death drive is characterized by retreat from investment in the outside world, with energy directed only toward the self, ultimately toward not thinking, not moving, ultimately to death as an end.

The life instinct, on the other hand, was a protean potential that realized its pulsation through combinatory migration: moving through the object world bringing diverse dimensions into dialectical fruition with one another. In social terms, the life instinct would have to be inclusive because its instinct is to find and engage all objects no matter what.

If together we run into beautiful worlds that have cherry-picked reality, we are buried above ground without even knowing it.

We are avoiding "commerce," a word I have a special fondness for.

We help ourselves if we understand that the genius of commerce is not simply in economic profit, but in the act of commerce itself. The trade routes by sea of the fourth century from Sumeria (and in China and India) brought people into relation to one another: not through ideology or religion, but through trade. If we understand that "a trade route is a logistical network identified as a series of pathways and stoppages used for the commercial transport of cargo" then those interested in the neuroscience of the brain and unconscious thinking see a rather stunning parallel in the logic of pathways endemic to *commerce*.

The first definition of the word "commerce" is an "activity that relates to the buying and selling of goods and services." And the second definition? "Social intercourse: interchange of ideas, opinions, or sentiments."

And as we know, not long after the trade routes were established, driven by the market, that inevitable phenomenon followed soon after: *tourism*! People wanted to see the places where these precious newfound goods came from; they were curious about these odd lands with wonderful objects. The tourists might be insulted to be termed "adventurers" or "explorers" and okay, they did many other things than simply see the sights.

Markets exchange goods, but then people meet and exchange ideas. People meet people to buy and sell. People meet people to meet people and countries: tourism.

So those developing the compound syndrome are not engaging in commerce but retreating from it even as they accumulate capital. And they offer us a vision of "life" that seems on the face of it admirable. We can—it is suggested—accumulate vast sums of wealth and fund other people's lives (their commerce) and yet we foment an aim that such commerce should hopefully result in retreat into the gated community, or the mausoleums of wealth.

If global commerce retains its interpersonal vitality, it will bring people together in fruitful ways beyond their local imaginations and the limited logic of capital. But the accumulation of wealth for its own sake fosters enclaves of the wealthy that become like clotted objects impeding and not helping the flow of commerce.

That is, as the great commercial pioneers retreat into enclaves—even consoling themselves by becoming great philanthropists—their contribution always was in their commercial creativity: their ability to bring ideas into the marketplace and to vitalize it. We need to make no moral judgment about capitalism here, but we can observe that from a psychological point of view the accumulation of wealth destroys the life instincts endemic to commerce and its protean ramifications.

Even though Buffet, Gates, Zuckerberg, and others finance new projects and make inventive creativity possible, they are not parallel governments and would not, I am sure, see themselves as undermining representative democracy by operating parallel governments.

Countries around the world—and we only need to look at Greece and the United States—suffer infrastructure neglect due to a comparative poverty of wealth necessary to operate a nation-state. Just as we need creativity in the commercial market, we have to vitalize the marketplace we term international political relations, that themselves are funded by the political efficacy of their nation states. To create parallel national and international governments may work in the short run but it will drain political capital and international relations in ways that will ultimately destroy the commercial market as well.

I do not think the above highly gifted people understand that as role models for many in the global community they are sustaining an anti-commercial ideal that leads people into the compound syndrome. Nor do I think they comprehend that in doing so they are unwittingly offering the world a picture of a parallel reality to the actual world, in which one can indeed live in heaven on earth if the financial gods (the idealized marketplace) can deliver one through the pearly gates of the compound. I do not think they understand that in offering a parallel reality they are also setting up parallel governments—or, national and international organizations that govern much of the world without accountability to the electorates. I do not think they intend at all to defeat representative democracies. I do think they are not thinking and not thinking *enough* about the implications of one's way of life—conveyed to one's children, to one's community—which is a feature of normopathic life and of the compound syndrome.

In the seminar at the end of this week, I will suggest ways in which we can meet the challenges of the new era without ego deformation, but that is a different topic. Now we focus on the implications of ego change for management, for regional relations, and for differing forms of communication. It would be a logical development of this change that human beings will be less inclined to make stand-alone decisions (that exemplify the history of leadership) as the morphogenesis of new ego forms demands that any leader be clearly a part of the picture and thus, inevitably, less capable of separation from the world of production—enabling him or her to objectify things—and more an unconscious spokesperson for the market.

That is, the history of "top-down" decision making will be (and is) challenged by the sheer speed and density of the globalized community. Those CEO's who are committed to their organizations are understandably both increasingly anxious about how to make crucial decisions within the mix of lightning-quick commerce and we are seeing increasing anxiety about making decisions leading to a form of "delegation displacement" in which the hope (or demand) is that decisions can be formed from appointed senior executives when in fact this is a case of "displace the anxiety onto someone else." And the long tradition of CEO departure—the revolving door executive—is an attractive pre-arranged flight pattern for some executives. Companies that have a relatively high turnover of CEO's or senior executives may be trying to adapt to the impossibility of the top-down structure in today's world, although shareholders, stakeholders, and others cannot understand much less empathize with the huge burden on a CEO.

Most importantly, in my view, both for purposes of our creative and non-subordinate relation to our new technologies (or new era as I refer to it), we have to develop new forms of leadership, ones that reward selves (and organizations, countries, etc.) for group-driven decision making. That is, the usual top-down management structure (be it CEO, president of a country, head of an NGO) is not simply dated: it is hazardous. The decisions we make—across the board—have to utilize not simply forms of social democracy but I would put it differently: forms of intellectual democracy where we pool mental capabilities to form high-functioning units able to cooperate across intersecting contextual realities or what I term intersecting contextual realities (ICR).

The solution to the unconscious death drive of the compound syndrome is to grasp the life instinct of commerce and to enable human beings in organizations to access parts of the mind that are profoundly able to perceive, process, and recreate reality within the world, not in the anodyne simulation of heaven upon earth, but in the real world. To do so will take a sea change in our understanding of the human mind, especially the unconscious mind, and that topic we take up this weekend.

4 Unconscious Thinking

Psychoanalytical thinking is concerned largely with unconscious processes, in the individual or the group. Our unconscious mind is much more complex and quick-moving than consciousness and if we take the time to learn how to use it we will grow our minds—almost with an evolutionary bent. This is one way we can keep up with the complex forms of communication and organization that we have created.

The focus this weekend will be on how we can utilize unconscious thinking to perceive, organize, and create ideas within the fast-breaking world of the IT era. If the twenty-first century is, as proclaimed, a giant step forward in the way we communicate—such that the human being is meant to be displaced by AI—this could only become so if we ignore our unconscious mind which may have been dormant for millennia, as we have neglected one of our greatest gifts.

I am going to concentrate on the psychology of the workplace and how to introduce new practices designed to develop unconscious thinking. For the sake of time I will imagine a conventional setting—a corporation that produces products that must be cutting edge in a highly competitive universe—but tomorrow we will look at other organizations and what we can bring to them from a psychological perspective.

The model proposed here is clearly suited to an organization that is already fairly enlightened and ready to maximize its creative potential.

The focus in these two lectures will be on the creative production of ideas and not on issues of management or the internal operation, per se, of an organization. Our focus presupposes an organization seeking to maximize its product creativity by developing new connections to the stream of ideas that tend to invent the future.

The model to be discussed in these seminars, however, can be adapted to other uses—other than simply the production of ideas for products and so forth—but these other uses will be taken up during the discussion.

Much of what I will say indicates the need for a rather radical alteration in our understanding of ourselves. Many of our assumptions about how to problem-solve organizational issues are either outdated or simply wrong. In turn, the means by which we can transform our capabilities have always been hiding in plain sight. So, as we explore matters, I will be bringing perfectly common and well-known phenomena into the light of day and indicate how employing them will enhance our skills.

Whether you work in government, in regional organizations, corporations, or the world of international finance, all of us exist in differing forms of social organization that are "top-down." To simplify, a company will usually have a Board of Directors, a CEO, a CFO, and different heads of departments. It will have a history of either manufacturing or providing a service and each year it will aim to do better than the previous year. In a way, history keeps the present to account.

Organizations thus usually set "targets" to improve a product or a service. They evaluate "performance" and make adjustments to their processes in order to improve both the product and the performance. Whatever group a company forms to design or improve its product, usually the organization will set up a chain of responsibility that places very high emphasis on consciousness. Any group given a task will meet to think about the object presented to them, will discuss how things can be improved, and will seek to implement the improvement.

If a company is stuck, organizations will usually hire consultants who will implement their own system of evaluation to determine why the organization is under-performing. The consultants may issue a white paper with specific recommendations, or they may be employed only by senior management and their recommendations will be considered over time.

Indeed, a consultant or coach may work for quite some time to help senior executives come to terms with an evaluation that may be challenging in all sorts of ways. Those of you here have studied the many types of challenges to be expected either as consultants, coaches, or as managers as you face the age-old dilemma of coping with the variables of human personality.

Increasingly, we see organizations using a rather more horizontal approach to thinking than the top-down delegated one. It is more common, now, to have less structured meetings with only a rather broad brief (like "what can we do to improve our product"), with no one chairing the meeting, and with a cross-section of staff engaged in a free-floating brainstorming session.

By getting as many heads together in the room to think about things, the chances are that more ideas will be produced than in a more top-down targeted meeting. The downside might be a group experience of mental blood letting in which the after effects are a sense of chaos and uncertainty. Organizations like to feel they have a sense of direction, and that may not be the outcome of horizontal group thinking.

A private equity firm evaluating a prospective company will delegate tasks to its employees—some will vet the financial history, others will study the structure of the organization, and others will examine the ins and outs of the specific product—and a team will then meet to make a decision. Do we put capital into this firm and partner with it, or do we decline and move on? If we are bidding for a firm, how much do we offer?

It is this latter question—"how much money?"—that is not only bracing but also potentially paralyzing. We might think of it as the ultimate question, a moment of reckoning. So, let's note that there comes a time when time itself steps in and mandates a decision, one in which any group process must stop and something has to be written on the bottom line. With this in mind—the shadow of the final moment looming in the future—what can an organization do to maximize its thought process in order to be more prepared for this day than otherwise?

5 The Focus Group

Before we consider how unconscious thinking can be creative, let's remind ourselves of how groups usually try to solve a problem relating to production or business matters.

A focus group tasked with doing just that—narrowing in on the variables that contribute to the issue under discussion—will utilize that anxiety that rather naturally arises from the pressure put on the group by the problem itself. Anxiety—of the alarm bell type—concentrates attention, often rids the group of impediments to consciousness (such as rivalries between departments or people) because the problem has to be solved, all the way round, in order to "move forward."

The "harnessing" of anxiety—taking it from the problem and transforming it into a group trying to solve that problem—is and always will be a crucial feature of human organizational life. This anxiety—much like "signal anxiety" in the individual—fires the brain cells, stimulates thought and discussion, and often drives a solution to the problem.

Anxiety-based group thinking is perhaps the most useful way for any group to solve problems arising from "the immediate." People who are good at "trouble shooting" are valuable members of any group because they have the ability to focus on the relevant issues and—as importantly—to discard the tertiary, thus helping colleagues to save time and not be distracted.

But if the problem arising is not from "the immediate" and the group has been enduring it for months or longer, then anxiety is not only no longer productive but it is now counterproductive. Instead of firing the brain and inspiring mental solutions to the problem, chronic anxiety has the opposite effect; indeed, it now breeds its own form of depression (due to the failure of thought) that makes group meetings counterproductive.

In the twenty-first century, the sheer pace of events (geopolitical, economic, social media, etc.) means that even a skilled focus group trying to manage the anxiety of imminent failure may be stymied and overwhelmed.

Although we seem determined to hand over much of our ability and functioning to AI, such outsourcing carries unknown hazards even if we can see the benefits. Not the least of our concerns should be that at a time when we need to employ relatively unused parts of our brain, outsourcing that task to AI will—over time—further degrade our capabilities and almost certainly compromise the species.

This concern is not mine alone: far from it. Fortunately, thousands of people involved in planning within a wide range of organizations are concerned about the problem posed by our retreat into mental enclaves bolstered by dependence on prosthetic devices that are meant to serve us, as we no longer serve ourselves. Thus, it is important that we tolerate this angst—it is collective signal anxiety—so we can begin to shape our future.

As I hope to illustrate, one method of problem-solving (or thinking within organizations) is not only indirect but seemingly counterintuitive. Rather than focusing on a problem, the indirect approach is to relax and simply allow whatever thoughts cross the mind to emerge. If you see in this method the practice principles of psychoanalysis—in which a patient approaches his problems by casting them out of mind simply to report apparently irrelevant ideas to the analyst—then you would be correct. Freud's invention was for the individual. Since his era, many analysts—especially Bion, Jacques, Mengies-Lyth, and Gordon Lawrence—have extended the psychoanalytical process to group and organizational thinking. And as you know, your program here—at INSEAD—sustains and grows that tradition in unique and valuable ways.

So, in the spirit of the indirect approach, let me digress.

6 Take a Hike

Imagine that right now I said to you that we are going to take a break of about seventy minutes or so. Imagine I asked each of you to turn off your cell phones and go for a walk outside of this building. You would have to walk alone.

After a while, some of you would be rather lost in thought. Ideas you did not know that you had would suddenly just pop into mind. Some of you would be imagining your workplace but now transformed by new ideas that would be unsettling but innovative. The phrase "I never dreamed this could be the case" might have a new resonance to it.

By providing the image of taking a walk, I am also borrowing an observation from psychology that when people just go for a walk—not from point A to B—as in just amble about looking at things, they naturally get lost in thought. Wordsworth walked some 20,000 miles in his lifetime, and when walking, he "wrote" many of his poems. Rousseau said, "I have to walk in order to think," and he was the first Western figure who connected walking to thinking.

The psychoanalyst and infant observer, Daniel Stern, observed that those infants who were presented with "novel objects" developed curiosity and became brighter and more innovative than infants and children who were coddled in a routine.

Some routines, however, have a high degree of variability in them. When I go for a walk near my farmhouse in North Dakota, I will follow a traditional course—usually across my meadow to my dirt road, up to the gravel road, and then one of three directions along other roads, so it seems predictable. But I never know what I will see. Perhaps deer, often differing raptors, on occasion the eagles, or an owl. In other words the natural world changes. Also, there is something about embodied thinking—the walking of a walk—that I believe guides us into deeper levels of day dreaming, rather like climbing into a soft bed in a sleepy frame of mind augurs a good night's sleep.

So, what might this teach us?

Those of us in organizational life need to know how to tap human creativity, in particular, unconscious processes. The studies I have discussed point to a need for organizations to create "down time" in which staff can—well—just wander off into daydreaming on the job or being encouraged to get out of the office to go for a walk. Some might jump to the image of an exercise room and treadmills, with heads plugged into an iTunes playlist. However nice and efficacious this is, it is more of a production line in which the self is fed a program in which the goals set by the routine—the number of minutes meant to be on the treadmill with the number of miles meant to be run—is perhaps creatively counterproductive. That is, we may be setting analogues to the ordered and over-structured self that deters wandering. One must keep in mind that if we step off the treadmill we risk serious injury.

Companies often go on retreats to a rural area, which is quite wise but also telling. There is something about being housed inside a highly structured and overly familiar universe that dulls the mind. Some of the more creative companies seem to have cottoned on to the vitality of the natural world and have housed themselves on the edge of a city, near a wild area or park where employees can ramble.

One of the things I loved about being a student at UC Berkeley was the numerous groves and hills on the campus, as it climbed up the hills and overlooked the San Francisco Bay. It was inspiring.

But what do we do with these observations?

First, we have to allay anxiety. What we are to talk about is not intended to replace traditional top-down forms of organization or focus group forms of thinking. We need these traditions for reasons we may come to during the discussion.

This said, in the twenty-first century especially, we have to use the remarkable intelligence of the human brain—which "thinks" in its own way hundreds of ideas a second—and generates the unconscious mind. We may never know exactly the connection between brain and mind, but it is fair to say that unconscious thinking depends on neural pathways and the vast storehouse of the brain with its capacity to make endlessly new connections to the stimuli evoking it.

We now know that dreaming at night and dreaming by day access deeper levels of mental life and are more creative than the linear lines of consciousness. You will see that I have already made a recommendation to all of you in the room. Find a way to help those in organizational life take a good long walk—alone—every day or so. Think about changing a lunch break into something more like a picnic in which people can take a sandwich with them on their walk. Get them out of their workspace so that they can return revitalized rather than sleepy because blood has rushed to their stomach (the lunch effect) and will now dull the brain.

7 The Work Place and the Work Day

Consultants and coaches, when visiting an organization should look at the physical environment of the workspace. Become environmental psychologists and take note of the "workplace" as a form of holding environment as Winnicott put it. Many office places are deadly even if they seem glorious. For example, a large open plan office with glass panels may seem to be a good idea but it may cramp the human need for a form of privacy essential to creative thinking. I cannot go into this further now, but you get the idea and can come up with your own notions for discussion.

Now let's turn to another specific recommendation.

The best time to use the group process is after the individual walk. This too is a complex psychological phenomenon, but in short, people have arrived at work in the morning, let's say, and have "had a glance" at the day's work. They are several hours into working and may have been in a meeting or two already, and so forth. Then the walk-break takes them completely away and is time to get lost in thought. It is upon return that the organization can tap the creative potential of this moment.

I will return to this in a moment when discussing the reverie group.

Today I want to sketch the broad outline.

The best time of day for a top-down meeting is at the end of the day. If management needs to convene for performance discussion it should be then because these will be higher stress moments and human beings need to feel they can escape the duress. Although the meeting may stimulate anxiety in the day and intrude upon the wandering mind, the self knows that it will be in the car, or on the train, headed home and to relief soon enough. Best to let staff then "sleep on it"—on whatever came up in the top-down meeting—and to arrive at work the next morning to just get on with things.

Mornings are not a good time for staff meetings, although many top-down organizations do convene first thing in the morning. Unfortunately, this breaks the psychological momentum of "sleeping on it"—on the efficacy of dreaming as problem-solving—and on the need to enable this form of creative thinking (the dream) to link up first thing in the morning with the self's mental creativity in the office space.

Let's step back a moment and review the workday following the above changes. What does a dream team do?

It begins around 3 p.m. on Day 1 when the team holds a meeting where what I will term a Shared Object of Thought (SOOT) is provided. One person is tasked with finding a SOOT and pitching it to the group. He is called a pitcher and the act is that of pitching.

Then the group disbands, and after returning to their offices they head home. The issues raised in the meeting—and the SOOT—will be circulating in minds, but each person will have touched base in his or her office before going home.

On the drive home, or tram or train or bus, each person will naturally be lost in thought, although it is fair to say that people are already beginning to work on the SOOT. At home, if they have a spouse or family they may talk about this week's SOOT. "Off piste" conversations are kosher and indeed a member may talk with a friend or two just to kick ideas around. The only prohibition is that they cannot discuss their ideas with people at work.

Then that night they sleep and hopefully both dream and can recall their dreams.

The following morning they proceed on yet another journey, back to work. They will return to reverie-by-car (etc.), but when they cross the threshold into the work space they will go to the office and get to work. In so doing, whatever reveries they have been having will now be superseded by the portfolio of consciousness and focus.

Then comes the lunch break, a walk, and participation in a unique form of group process, which we shall term a Reverie Group (RG). (I will return to this momentarily.)

When Freud studied dreams, he made a few crucial observations.

During the "dream day"—the day before the dream—the self engaged in all kinds of activities. Some of the events would prove to have a "high psychic value" and they would compete to be in the dream that night. Then the self would go off to sleep and dream. The next day the self might recall the dream events and they might naturally lead to associations. Freud exploited this natural feature of our psychology to situate psychoanalysis at the intersection of conscious remembering and unconscious reception, a collaboration essential to learning from the dream of the night. (Free association as a process is a blending of unconscious and conscious "reflection.")

Before the RG, the subject will go for a walk. He will now be recollecting the SOOT and some of his free associations. He will know from experience that the walk is meant to be a *meandering* as psycho-somatic preparation for the RG that takes place shortly. He enters the room, sees his fellow group members, and they all sit in their chairs. Someone will begin talking, followed by another, and another, and so it goes.

It may be that any organization only needs an RG meeting once a week. The time in between meetings is important to individual creativity, as of course it is to collective benefit.

Thus the RG "dream day"—if we like—begins with an evocative object, followed by several *differing types* of unconscious idioms: thought by routine travel, thought at dinner time, thought by relaxed conversation, thought by dreaming, thought by the associative aftereffects of the dream, thought by morning work objects, thought by a deliberate praxis of walking aimed at setting a mood for reverie, thought by group process, thought by reflection.

This model builds on Freud's observations, but as can be imagined the process he observed is intensified and brought into the life-stream of an institution. Whereas before the dreamer would make his own journeys to an analysis, here he is heading to the work space, sharing his inner process with his colleagues who pool their dreams and reflections.

We note that the differing forms of unconscious thought—by travel, dinner time, etc.—*subject* the SOOT to many layers and types of thinking. Ordinary spaces and times are exploited to serve the purpose of unconscious thinking. We build on Freud's intuition that the day residue is crucial, but now we arrange for that day to be even more evocative.

Much will, of course, be left up to chance, but equally, we will plant the seeds of the evocative into the minds of the individuals and the group, thus developing both the forms of unconscious thinking and the yield of the content.

There must be a break between reverie and reflection, and this is simply accomplished by a routine in which all members stand and perhaps stretch for a minute or so before sitting. The aim is obvious: to enlist the body and embodiment as a means of assisting the mental lives of the participants. As you will be realizing, a vital part of the success of unconscious thinking is taking a break from a fixed situation.

It is important *to include the body and the somatic* in thought processes. A simple "break" in which people stand up and stretch—that takes one minute—is invaluable. But we neglect our bodies, ignore our soma, and suffer unnecessary impoverishments as a result.

8 The Dream Team

So, now to the reverie work group or the dream team.

Imagine the group functioning within an institution where the employees work 9:00 a.m. to 5:00 p.m. Later, we will see how it could be used in other sectors.

The RG may seem like a contradiction. How can you be in a state of reverie and also work at the same time?

If the work is unconscious and the self is relaxed enough to be in reverie, then the two belong together.

A dream team could be eight or more people who meet once a week. The participants will have common tasks and intersecting projects, but an RG can only function if people simply say what has crossed their mind. Let's assume that the group is working on a project—it does not matter what it is—and that the evocative topic of the day or week was pitched the previous day at the end-of-day meeting.

We see that this is a two-day weekly process: the RG meeting receiving a SOOT and the meeting next day in which associations are shared. Keep in mind that the number of people involved is very small and that the remainder of the staff are not involved. So, the group is not personnel or time-consuming and hardly ostentatious. They have, therefore, a shared object of thought (SOOT).

Now, how do we pitch to the dream team?

Clearly, the SOOT must be evocative. The value of the pitcher cannot be underestimated. We do not have time to explore this important function but needless to say one could spend many hours going over the phenomenology of a SOOT aimed to be evocative as well as discussing and assessing the abilities of pitchers. You will know something about people who pitch films to producers. They have a few minutes to present an evocative and moving image in the minds of a group of people. How effective they are in their evocative capability will determine whether the film goes to the next stage or dies there.

(It will be clear to the group who the gifted pitchers are.)

You will have received a brief SOOT from me in "Park With Us." (A document circulated to the group and discussed on pages xx-xxx.) It should be evocative and lead one to differing ideas, perhaps many of them having nothing to do with parking at all.

If so, your lines of thought give you some idea of the associative process evoked by an intriguing SOOT.

After this meeting today, see if you can come up with a SOOT for your client or your organization, one you could pitch to your "dream team."

After the SOOT is announced, the RG will head home.

Back at work the next day, they will have slept on it, returned to the solitude and concentration of work life, and just had a walk. All participants will know that the conscious SOOT—shared in the RG—is in the background and sometime since then, but probably while walking, seemingly irrelevant ideas will pop up. During this meeting, individuals should just report their passing thoughts.

Let's pitch a few SOOTs your way.

You are consulting for L'Oréal. They target a certain market, and it is fair to say this is for the well-to-do. You are aware, however, that perfume and cologne in centuries past—before modern hygiene—was a crucial way for people to deter bacteria and to prevent the spread of disease. So, a consultant and an RG group are in place at L'Oréal and here is the pitch: "Many in the world are afraid of Zika, West Nile Fever, and other mosquito-borne diseases. Mosquito repellants do not sell because they emit an unpleasant odor. Enter L'Oréal." If you work with L'Oréal and you hear this and your Idea Quotient is high, members of the group will start free associating and in a relatively short time many ideas will have been produced.

But that pitch is rather a "lob": almost a gift in a way.

Here is another one. Basically just two words: "INSEAD and the Tokyo Olympics." It might be hard to see how an INSEAD group would work with these two ideas but a good dream team would easily start generating ideas that would benefit INSEAD.

A SOOT is only as good as its evocative power. If you have a rather hard time doing this, do not worry. But ask a friend or partner or spouse to see what they can do with your task. See who is a natural born pitcher. Finding a great pitcher or two makes you a gifted scout and of considerable value in your own right to any client or organization.

9 How Does This Actually Work?

An RG should be ninety minutes. The first sixty minutes should be free association amidst reverie and the remaining thirty minutes should be the period of reflection. The first sixty minutes are given over to unconscious thinking in a rambling mélange; the next thirty with reflections by the participants following the comment of the group leader.

(The group leader will be an expert in the RG and will remain in place until the group is able to lead itself.)

For the first sixty minutes, the group simply listens to any person's passing comments. If they respond it must be only as an association and not as a dialogic opportunity. No one is to comment analytically or otherwise on any person's musings.

After a while, you want a group to respond to an evocative object in a free associative way.

The group leader, functioning much as a psychoanalyst would, will listen to the associations during the period of reflection. He or she may identify patterns of thought or may remain silent other than to intervene when the group violates the protocol. (A violation, for example, would be when one member engages another in dialogue or when a member asks how they can make sense of what they have been saying.)

Freud's theory of unconscious thinking was that the most significant ideas were always those that initially proved to be seemingly quite irrelevant. In time, those ideas would link up in a chain of associations and an unconscious idea would be revealed through the chain.

In subsequent meetings, the person who presented an irrelevant idea may follow it with seemingly other irrelevant ones, or, if one member has been inspired by the thoughts of another and this crosses the mind in the meeting, then it is fair for that other person's contribution to be referenced *if* it is part of a psychic genera. (We will discuss genera later.)

In a monologue, a person can be free associating. Almost certainly. A reason not to interrupt a speaker is that speaking is an act of transference if we understand that the transfer is from unconscious thoughts toward consciousness revealed in time through the deployment of the pattern or logical chain.

Ordinarily, if you interrupt a speaker while in the act of this transference you break the chain.

This is why when person A is free associating in monologue and person B interrupts him, the possibility of free associative thought may be broken. B interrupts A's chain with his own thoughts. A will often say "oh . . . where was I?" and may continue but will have lost the thread of thought.

On the other hand, it is important for a group—when seeking to develop a group mind—to swap seeming monologues. How is this done? By the fact that at no time does anyone in the group question another or ask for an explanation. Anyone can say what he/she thinks but it should not be an act of *corrective* interruption aimed at formenting dialogue. Speakers need to attune their individual unconscious to the group, one that will take some months of practice but the group will evolve. Thus, when it meets someone will kick it off and talk a bit and then stop. Someone else will pick it up and then stop.

But . . . there are moments—many of them—when a speaker will follow a line of thought and stop, and person B will pick it up and A will then have a sudden inspiration. It can only happen when B has begun to speak and A suddenly realizes something. These Eureka moments are creative interruptions and A's comment depends on "the period of hesitation" that has taken place and can only be facilitated by dialogical interruption.

But the interruption is voluntary in that A has decided to stop talking and B is probably just involved in "a relay" race of sorts in which the baton is passed to him/her for a moment. Call this the "baton pass," which is understood as facilitative of A's riffing. Thus, the pair is involved in cooperating as a conscious couple in the facilitation of free association, or unconscious thinking.

If I ask someone in the group to say anything to me, chances are I will hear it and then briefly look away, or up to the ceiling. We all do this. What are we doing? We are *transferring* the two-person verbal exchange into a one-person thought world.

As with the Winnicott baby and period of hesitation—where the baby turns away from spatula in order to think—when we look away we are *creating thought*.

We are making what the person said into our saying, into a thought. Before, it was a speech content, part of the other's narrative. It was the others. Now we make it our own. We may pass it back to the other who will, in turn, have to turn away and make it their own.

This baton passing is crucial to the dialectic of relational creativity, which rests on a paradox that for two people to be inter-subjective, they must allow one another to be deeply individuated in the process, to take a mental content and distort the other's words or train of thought, into one's own train of thought. In time, what is disrupted in consciousness starts to become linked by unconscious communications—like in jazz—and the two develop a language that is only possible between two people, after each has destroyed the seeming integrity of a sensible two-person discussion.

We can see that a meeting trying to stop time and thought in the interests of a unit of agreement is actually is ordinarily counterproductive.

Our prejudice against one person just going on and on is an impatience with unconscious life itself. Indeed, even a boring person who seems to be droning allows us time to drift off in thought but actually to be connected, and it is out of this boredom that sudden thoughts can arise.

Each person in a group plays a vital function. It may be that one person is creatively boring, but his/her soporific is useful to the more active unconscious minds in the group. But the contentious argumentative person who wants to nail down reason or common sense is destructive of the group process and must be asked to leave.

All the above will be taking place in the RG where there is an analytically trained and informed person. The leader and the group will know that thoughts spoken by one person will usually be usually responded to in no obvious way. If staff are trained in this model of thinking then it will matriculate into decision making realms and a CEO, for example, may come to appreciate that "off the wall" first responses to what he or she says—which in the past would have seemed almost offensively blind to what has just been said by the CEO—are in fact unconscious uses of the object: the object being what the CEO has just said. In other words, this period of hesitation, vital to some deeply creative first responders will be allowed and understood for what it is.

10 An Example
Perfume in the Jungle

There are two distinctive formats for a free-associating group. One is indirect, the other is direct. I will begin with the indirect approach.

So, let's use L'Oréal.

Eight people have been in the room, and during the first sixty minutes, the following non sequiturs were stated. Each person speaking is given a number (1–8) and here is how some of the thoughts might have been uttered:

(3) "I imagine a little girl in a village in Africa somewhere and she loves the scent of banana, and I see a commercial of a banana floating through the air" . . . (8) "I had a dream last night that pops into mind, of sitting in an airport lounge waiting for my airplane but then I see there is a long gang plank leading to a ship and I wonder how that is going to take off" . . . (6) "An image of a glass of sparkling Rose from just outside of Nice comes to mind" . . . (7) "I see my mother washing bed clothes in a very old tub with a roller for drying them" . . . (3) "I keep thinking of the banana but the sound is more important: as in 'na na'" . . . (5) "I'm thinking of whether I left the keys in my car or whether they are in the drawer of my office." (2) "I read in the paper yesterday that Donald Trump said he could easily imagine having sex with his daughter and would, only he couldn't because of course he is the father" . . . . (8) "I'm thinking of the plank that goes to the ship and it brings to mind the long planks that were vertical, I guess in WW1, where people sort of had to ascend" . . . (2) "a phrase comes to mind—'when the going gets tough, the tough get going'" . . . (7) "I imagine a car going down Route 66 which I think is in the USA somewhere" . . . (1) "I remember when I was about seven—this has been in my mind the last few minutes—that we took a trip to Vancouver and went on these ferry boats and the captain asked me to take the helm but I could not see over the rim of the handle so had no idea where we were going." (7) "I" . . .

Now, I am not going to continue with this invented group. We would have to multiply this considerably to fill the hour. But I want you to see what such a group might "look like." You will see that although the group has been given a SOOT only one member of the dream team has actually alluded to it thus far: the first speaker. The others seem not to mention it at all. But the line of thought—the links connected by the non sequiturs—will be this group's unconscious thinking about the SOOT. Indeed, some of the associations—at an airport with a ship outside, of a WW1 plank going up, of a ferry boat where a kid cannot see above the wheel—may indicate that the SOOT is unconsciously perceived at this point as an idea that is not in the right place or requires more mental maturity for the dream team to ponder before actual ideas of how to use the object are produced.

However, paradoxically, even though the group of thinkers seems to suggest that the idea is out of reach there is a high degree of productivity amongst the team and so the SOOT is highly evocative even if it seems to evoke cautionary notes.

Now let's turn to the direct free associative group. This follows Freud's *The Interpretation of Dreams* in that the *dream text* is the continual source of reference. It is the evocative object (SOOT), and it will be one of the functions of the group leader to recurrently remind the group of the SOOT in order to enhance evocative free association. To remind you, the SOOT is "L'Oréal and Mosquito repellent."

(3) "I imagine a film of a hoard of drone mosquitos targeting a joyful wedding group but as they get closer to the target they see a L'Oréal mosquito perfume bottle on a table and turn back" (1) "I am thinking of how you would apply it all over the body, or, well, just on the arms, neck, hands . . . ." (5) "A sound has just come to mind: Whooosh." (8) "My first thought was of a woman smacking mosquito's on her arm and then an immediate follow up of her putting on a small drop of the perfume and humming." (3) "I imagined a gorgeous typical L'Oréal model who puts on the mosquito repellant and whilst it drives the mosquitos away at the same time it draws incredibly handsome blokes." (8) "That leads me to think of driving them off!"

(4) "Men are the mosquitos!" (1) "Yeah, a L'Oréal woman is sort of driving them off and attracting them at the same time!!" [laughter, then silence]. (6) "I imagine a beautiful pregnant woman putting the perfume on her belly and the image is of her protecting herself and her baby but also of being very alluring and her husband or partner smells the wonderful scent and comes to be with them." (8) "A different kind of attraction, a different kind of sexy." (3) "I have just had a sort of sound image in my head of running water . . ."

(7) "That brings to mind sweating due to running, but an image of a really slender long-distance runner comes to mind . . ." [silence of a few minutes]. (3) "An image of turning up the earth comes to mind . . ." (7) "I am just wondering now about a field of flowers and honey bees and the image of the perfume on the body, and how a bee is such a beautiful little thing whilst a mosquito is so menacing . . ." [silence].

We see from the above that this group is directly focused on the concept of L'Oréal coming up with an approach to selling mosquito repellent. One has to imagine that after sixty minutes of this they will have produced scores of associations which is a considerable pool of knowledge (POK). It is highly likely that after the group breaks up as members go back to work, drive home later, have dinner, that what Freud termed "Einfall"—free associations that drop in from the blue—will come to mind. They are likely to be memorable and notable and individual members will no doubt write them down. If in a week's time—when the group meets again, they come to mind then they will enter the POK. The group will start to form clear sets of ideas that might spring genera.

11 Assessing an Organizations' Psychological Capability

How does a consultant determine if an organization can use an RG?

The consultant visits the workplace or institution and simply wanders about. His task is to form an RG but at the same time to collect evocative objects: topics that are within the lingo of the culture, which can be put vividly to stimulate thought.

After he finds two to five such topics, the prevailing management group meets and they go through an evaluation. Exactly as you would present a poem, you pitch an idea and see how the group thinks it (playing). From here, you can assess the group's creative level and potential and target its problems in the area of unconscious creativity.

Although this will be pitched to upper management in the first place, the consultant can assess from the group response whether the leadership can "play" with a SOOT, or whether it defends itself against this. A typical defense is contempt or ridicule.

During this visit, however, the consultant will have selected eight people to form a trial RG, and this will not ordinarily include senior management.

The rules will have been distributed and discussed in a meeting ahead of convening the RG. All participants must be given ample time to discuss the ground rules before convening a meeting.

The rules might read as follows:

1. The consultant will convene the group.
2. No questions can be posed to the consultant once the group convenes.
3. Each member is to simply state what crosses their mind as it does.
4. No analysis of one's thought is permitted.

5. Abstractions should be kept to a minimum.
6. No conversation can take place between group members.
7. The consultant is free to identify unconscious patterns of thought as they arise, or more commonly, during the reflective period. The ideas are thus *objectified and made available for consciousness and discussion.*

Unlike a Bion group or Tavistock group, the rules governing an RG are clear, written down, and disseminated in advance. In this respect, the process invokes Lacan's concept of the symbolic order that—in this particular group process—mitigates regression and more primitive functioning in the group. In particular, it prioritizes free association and the act of interpretation. As the task is clearly stated and the rules governing behavior also made clear the protocol functions as an evocative structure in its own right.

Interestingly, when members realize that the group process is not designed to evoke private views of one group member or another (and so forth), the negative effect of individual personality upon the functioning of a group mind is reduced to a minimum. Indeed, if it is clear that a person cannot adapt to the "rules of the game" then he or she will be asked by the consultant to leave the group.

To conclude, the consultant visits an organization to assess its overall level of creative functioning. This is assessed through observation of the work day and the idiom of the workforce. The consultant assembles an RG and assesses the ability of the staff to free associate. It is not difficult to determine the degree of freedom (to be unconsciously productive and creative) in these first meetings. If an organization is paralyzed and displays an unusual degree of paralysis, it is then the responsibility of the consultant to do a history of the organization in order to determine when, why, and how it has negatively impacted the capacity of the members to think freely.

Consultants will have a Quality Scale (1–100) to rate each sector of the organization, as well as the freedom of function found in the RG. Over time, the data from a QS of many different organizations will assist the consultant in noting any trends within types of organizations that should be objectified and considered.

For example, the QS found in automotive manufacturing may be high, but the QS in information technology industry is low. Or, if the QS is high in a certain sector—let's say the perfume industry—but low with a particular client, it will be the responsibility of the consultant to find which dimension of the organization is functioning below the average expected mark.

For example, the senior management may have a high QS score, but R&D (research and development) may be low. Groups will be rated but also the spaces between groups—such as the level of communication between, say, sales and marketing; or between senior management and product review—will be assessed.

The above assessment is standard and will be familiar to everyone. However, the assessment of unconscious thinking and creativity—discovered by convening RGs—will provide immediate evidence of the staff's capability.

12 Forming the Group Mind

We have discussed how an organization can arrange for an event that takes place over a twenty-four-hour period. It begins in the late afternoon with a group meeting in which an evocative object of thought is pitched, the self's brief return to office-base, the journey home, dinner and afterward with family or friends, the dreams in the night, the journey back to work, a concentrated period of work, the pre RG meandering walk, and then the RG. This sequence of events builds on Freud's theory of how we use dreaming and unconscious life but it takes the structure he employed and brings it into the workplace.

The dream team is not simply a collection of individuals. It is constituted in order to form a group mind: that is, a type of mind only possible within a highly functioning integrated group of people.

The sequence just mentioned *is a structure* not simply for thinking, but eventually, when it becomes part of one's mental assumption, it *forms a group mind*. This step aims to develop deep (and vast) unconscious processes of thought dedicated to the specific needs of the organization.

It is important to understand that the group is present and still functioning when all the individuals are off doing their own thing. Although the individual mind is such that we can forget about it—so it is as if we are not present when our unconscious thinking continues at its pace—knowing that we are part of a group mind means that participants can more deeply relax into the sense that they are part of a living matrix even in its absence. Further, the evidence in time that one perceives the group mind—and uses it—is an invaluable realization that empowers individuals, groups, and their organizations.

It will be evident that, however important the knowledge gained from this mindset is, the structure we have discussed—one *built into and derived from the ordinary routines of the work world*—will in-form all the structures of the workplace. So, when the organization convenes an afternoon meeting that is not devoted to the dissemination of a specific evocative object of thought (for the RG), the group mind that has been built and formed around that specific task will now approach all objects of thought with unconscious skills.

Further, even though journeys to and from work, or breaks in the day, will not be specifically devoted to a SOOT, the mind cultivated out of SOOT and for RG will be in place and will perceive all phenomena at the organization through the multilocular lenses of unconscious perception.

This hardly displaces consciousness nor indeed specific task designations or focal thinking. Rather, it provides an underlying depth of unconscious thought that simply provides consciousness with much greater information and a better structure for thinking. As discussed, I have termed this "dynamic consciousness"—rather what Damasio means by "extended consciousness"—to describe a consciousness that is also turned *inward* to receive the communications from unconscious perceptions and creativities.

Finally, the structure links the workplace with all other spaces in a self's life so that thinking at work is enriched by the thought processes at home, in the car, while reading a book, watching a cricket match, cooking dinner, or seeing a film. That is, the structure we have discussed—with its nodal point being the designated evocative object disseminated at the afternoon meeting—becomes a matrix with gravitational pull to it that will quite naturally (as in unconsciously astute) gather all information available to the individual self that will be pooled in the group.

Thus, the group will have formed a structure predicated on the psychic process I have termed "genera," and now we turn to this.

13 Creating Genera

Genera is a term I have coined to describe unconscious thinking that leads to creative new perspectives or ideas. It follows Freud's theory of how a dream forms at night, derived from events during the day, but ones that evoke one's entire psychic life and mental structures.

It borrows from Freud's theory of the life instinct—as a force within us that grows by combining "objects" of thought (procreatively so) and thus enlarges the self's abilities. If we think of the mind as "composed" of thousands of matrices of thought (Freud termed them "clusters of ideas"), each of which has its own gravitational field, then as we experience new phenomena and join them with what we know, we create new mental fields.

So, part of the function of the RG is to tap into this ordinary feature of creative mental life in order to grow the unconscious mind of the organization and to maximize the potential for the creation of genera.

We will see, however, how individual genera, when developed as a group process exploit the remarkable range and depth of unconscious processes. It increases the scope of genera to an incalculable extent. In particular, the critical function of genera—to serve as a matrix constituted out of the gravity of interest—once established, then taps into *the way unconscious creativity works*. Unconscious thinking is one thing; unconscious creativity is another.

The unconscious creativity that Freud sensed, in his theory of "clusters of thought" that form nuclei in the "system unconscious," is in fact a theory of how unconscious perceptions, interests, and the threads of unconscious disseminations received from *others* (other people, other organizations, society as other, culture as production of other thoughts) gradually *constellate* into one unconscious organization that *then* creates *its own perceptions and productions* based on its unique formation.

So, to iterate, if we now see how remarkably wide-ranging and deep this structure is once formed within an organization, we note that an RG is capable of processing and creating a form to deal with the intersecting contextual realities of the global world that move at lightning speed.

An RG is thus an evolutionary step in human mental life uniquely suited to the task of perceiving a more complex world. It is not difficult to see how organizations can profit (literally and figuratively) from the formation of the dream team. The study of this process—especially its capacity to generate mental holding areas to receive and recreate the data emerging from the global world—is of enormous potential.

Now, let's return to a few practical matters.

It takes about one year for a dream team to reach its potential.

And like most things of value in life, it does not come without a cost. A large organization that has a coach trained in RG would want this person to set up the groups to begin with. We can discuss this later, but in short, the pool of members would be sent a confidential questionnaire that would discern the best possible membership for a group. Not all people are suited to an RG, and those for whom this is not possible should not be pressed into it. And a questionnaire would determine who does not want to be in a room with whom.

It is more than possible that a good dream team can be self-sustaining over time because individual members will internalize the group leader's skills, and so the group also provides on-the-job training for its own consultancy.

In the early stages, a consultant will no doubt have to intervene if any group member seeks dialogue with others, or if a group member keeps nodding when another is speaking, or any number of "interactions" that warrant comment. A comment might be something like "The member is seeking to engage a colleague in conversation," which should be sufficient to alleviate the issue. Members might laugh in such moments—which is altogether understandable—but in time, members will appreciate that this is a "free-floating" form of thought. Knowing that one can speak one's mind without fear of judgment or oddly, without anticipation of its being overly welcomed leading to hypomanic mental activity, gradually informs the members that the value of the group is not in the production of single ideas but in the formation of a matrix that utilizes dreaming and day dreaming to constitute an unconscious mind that helps the organization.

Some might confuse this group with an AK Rice or Bion group, and that is understandable. But while those groups evoke anxieties and conflicts, the prohibition on dialogue within the dream team—as well as the rule that one cannot engage a colleague afterward to comment on his or her idea in the group—means that most of the problems generated by human personality will be marginalized in order that collective consciousness gradually comes to receive and to appreciate the receptive unconscious. In other words, the efficacy of the group as a thought process can be felt as a thing-in-itself that just seems to generate thought.

Dialogue *of sorts* does occur when any member in the group spontaneously recollects another member's contribution. A stream of consciousness is established—very much *as a stream* so that any members thoughts put into the stream may be picked up by any other member. This said, no speaker should expect that pursuant to his contributions there will be any follow-up at all. Indeed, in the beginning a consultant might say "The group feels that it must follow up any members comment."

But what about genera?

It will be a natural outcome of the process that seemingly all of a sudden, a member or two (or all of them) have an epiphany and find themselves with a completely new point of view about something. It may be about a product or a service, or a sales pitch. Whose idea was it? A member may suddenly come up with a groundbreaking idea, but the group will understand that this could not have taken place without the RG. Even the dreamer that night, or the self concentrating on work in the morning, or the walker just before RG, who has an inspired idea will not own it. It will have emerged from the culture of the group.

However, any RG *seeking* to be productive—to foster genera—will fail to do so. It is the responsibility of the consultant to point this out: "The group is struggling to come up with something"; or, "The group process is stuck celebrating what it thinks is a new idea."

But what if the idea really is new and members can hardly wait to announce the perspective to colleagues?

These seem perfectly natural aspects of human behavior, and that is rather the point.

Institutions will hardly achieve perfection in ridding themselves of the destructive sides of personality. But when considering the hazards of hubris with the RG, bear in mind that were this a "focus group" tasked with problem-solving that the group and the individual would be recalled in terms of the balance between the individual and the group contribution. The same is true of the RG.

After sixty minutes of free association and following a stretch break of a minute or so, the group now reflects on what has been said. The consultant will have tracked some of the free associations, and it will he his or her determination whether to start the period of reflective discussion.

This part of the work group is devoted to cultivating dynamic consciousness so that the many ideas generated are harvested for conscious consideration. If the group has been tasked by management to come up with a matrix of ideas after just one such meeting, it will be the responsibility of the consultant to report the ideas. It is more likely that a group will work on a SOOT for weeks or even months.

Some RGs will achieve harmony and others will not. There will also be many ways for a dream team's mental productivity to be made available to the larger group (i.e., the company or organization).

Perhaps you will see that the RG depends considerably on the individual in solitude. An RG could not possibly meet more than once a week and expect to be effective. Individuals will pool in the group but then meander between meetings. The walk is designed to give them a creative break in the hour preceding the RG, but the walk is also recommended as a daily creative break.

What about the many thoughts that arrive outside of the RG?

Should the more important ones not be written down? Wouldn't it be more productive to harvest those ideas as soon as possible by encouraging staff to share them with others in the organization?

That might seem sensible, and certain ideas will no doubt be lost given that they are not written down. But for an RG to develop, the members need to save the speaking of their ideas until the meeting. Keep in mind that this is a group devoted to unconscious work, so although conscious ideas will of course pop up and seem luminous, if they are of importance, they can wait until the meeting. Indeed, it is more likely that once the self knows that speaking the ideas happens in the RG, then for the most part the ideas will be saved for the group.

Nothing, however, prevents—nor should it!—the fact that each individual will use insights from this process during his or her workday. Whatever the designated job title and form of work ideas, that are relevant to the employee's task will emerge and be utilized. This is simply an outcome of the process.

14 The Value of Wisdom

Use the Elderly

The received wisdom that groups need new blood may be mitigated by the skills developed *over time* by long-standing members of the organizational community. The skill we discuss is the ability of an individual to be a creative member of a dream team. That skill is transmissible to others in the group, who will benefit, and it also contributes over the long run to the reputation of that dream team. Not only does this mitigate passing envy of a particularly creative person, but it also deepens the capability of all members who take increasing and appropriate pride in their group. It also obviously becomes noteworthy within the organization and speaks to the value of those who might otherwise be looking over their shoulders to the front door, wondering who might be coming in to replace them. The fear of obsolescence in the age of new technology is, of course, considerable. We see in the RG the value of wisdom, which is only possible through layers of experience over a long period of time.

15 The Pool of Knowledge and the Use of Culture

Over time, an RG will develop a POK. We have discussed how this grows its mind, but we turn now to its knowledge capital (KC).

The group's production of ideas we will term "pooling."

The consultant can note whether there is average, above average, or below average pooling on the day and note it as P, –P, or +P.

You will appreciate that by forming work groups from *within* organizations, by understanding the nature of unconscious perception, and the learning capital to be gained through submersion in culture, such working groups will *produce meaning*. The production of meaning is, arguably, our most important form of production. It *will* be profitable, but not at the expense of people. It will actually use our neurological banks, our individual and collective minds to *grasp reality, generate visions, and develop new forms of organization essential to our survival.*

The model of how to employ the free associative process has been limited in this lecture to a particular type of organization, one vested in producing goods or services for the present and the future. However, there are many adaptations to this process. Let me simply sketch a few so that you get the idea.

The use of culture.

Assume you consult with an NGO or a political entity (it could be the ministry in a country). A SOOT, then, would be any passing matrix of news that would stimulate wide-ranging thought. The pitcher will have read from several newspapers the day the SOOT is pitched. Whatever SOOT she picks will obviously be related to the culture of the organization.

Each organization is not only its own microclimate, but it is also its own microculture. Every organization must be subjected to a cultural analysis by any consultant who seeks to help it think creatively.

Once the culture is identified the links between its culture with the ICR's of the disparate cultures can be identified. A customary SOOT would be something in the news that is highly evocative. It remains simply for the pitcher to state this SOOT, and the group then goes home, and the work begins.

SOOTS derived from cultural dreaming—the ways in which differing societies, from a country to a region, to a profession, to a single organization, dream through "breaking news"—are invaluable. If your client is an organization dealing in a meaningful way with partner companies in different countries then your employees need to enter the stream of cultural thinking taking place in the partner countries. To do this, the culture has to become an embedded matrix in your own mind. To do this, you have to go to the country and live a week—or more—with a family. It may be better if they are not your business partners. (Think of student exchange or GAP year visits as the model.) These are not simply cultural exchanges, they allow people to internalize the paradigms of another culture and to begin to think within them.

If you create a meeting in another country, never meet in a hotel. That is a category error and from an unconscious point of view a malignant evocative object. Malignant because the ICR will be "processed" through the culture of The Four Seasons or wherever. If you meet in a five-star hotel, no one present is in touch with his or her own unconscious life. It is to thought what processed cheese is to the real thing. And many organizations—far more than they know—are suffering from processed thoughts sadly generated by living and thinking in an anodyne reality that becomes a malignant evocative object.

An alternative is to meet in someone's home in the country, where the meeting takes place. Families should be around—especially children—and people should mix business with family pleasure. I know this will seem highly odd, but what is strange is how infrequent this sort of meeting is. We do not learn from human experience; we seem opposed to our own benefits.

Even if the group has no specific developmental task (let's assume they make pipes for gas lines, etc.), remember, you are not simply problem-solving or even developing a product, you are teaching your workforce to develop unconscious skills. You are deepening and widening perception, but you are also accelerating it so that organizations can ride the wave of AI and not be submerged. The premise of this lecture is simple: the human mind and its brain are far more complex and nuanced than any AI could ever be. We are quite capable of developing a world to suit the human being but we will have to return to Freud and what he taught in order to rediscover something we noticed but did not use.

But unlike in Freud's time, we should be able to learn how to find highly evocative objects and how to stimulate our unconscious minds. He certainly taught us perhaps the most important such object: our dreams. And Gordon Lawrence followed in those footsteps, creating social dreaming groups that simply took one or another member's dreams and mulled them over.

16 The Logic of the Present

Given that the SOOT will be—at least unconsciously—a topic relevant to the organization (it is after all a work group), it *launches* "the logic of the present" or LOTP. This idea is not far off from Bohm's concept of "implicate logic" in that the free associations form a certain logic of thought, but why do I state they are the logic of the present?

The irony of unconscious thinking is that it ultimately displays a linearity of thought that is not only logical but also suggests further lines of thought—into the future.

Imagine you work for Boeing. You are a dream team set up to think about the prospect of drone aircraft. Your free associations have picked up the cultural resonances of "drone": drones as attacking terrorists, to drones as ironically threatening civil aviation. To drones as the play vehicles of the rich, famous, and drug addicted. You come up with "drone" as a synonym for tedious. The phrase "pilot less" or "self flying" aircraft raises negative associations until one in the group says, "I see a friendly face on the ground operating our airplane," and the group sees in its mind's eye "ground control" and the phrase itself is reassuring.

Time passes and the dream team comes up with a fabric of thought—a vision—that is not a form of advertisement or marketing, but a way for all in the industry to re-view and resituate the human being in an entirely new context. The aircraft is no longer piloted, but on each flight there is one pilot who knows the system and could step in in the event of any unforeseen event that for whatever reason seems to defy technology.

Let's call this "The Sully Factor" (named after the pilot who landed a disabled aircraft in the Hudson River) to imbricate into the future our need for a "transitional object," at least for some decades before new technology and a new generation truly makes this redundant. This is the result of thinking about the logic of the present which points toward future paths.

One of the crucial functions of the dream team is to set up the logic of that organization's present situation as it faces its tasks in order that the LOTP disseminates multiple vectors pointing to differing futures. All organizations, especially in the twenty-first century, have to use the LOTP in order to envision the immediate future (IF)—days or weeks—the near future (NF)—a matter of months and up to one year—the intermediate future (IMF) from one to five years—the decade future (DF) of ten years, and the long-term future (LTF). This topic is vast and way too complex to discuss today, as we have our hands full. But it is a vital function of organizations to utilize unconscious perceptions because dreams, daydreams, and free associative thinking provide an implicate logic that "sees into" all of the above *temporalities.*

Seeing into the future is an act of creation and, of course, is not akin to knowing what will happen in the future. But developing multiple lines of thought that organize many visions of the future is a vital task in today's world for obvious reasons.

For example, let me pitch the following:

"leisure travel."

What comes to mind as you think about this?

I expect that within a few hours, those of you attending this event will have come up with hundreds of ideas and visions. Were you to work together as a dream team you would form a POK and a mental structure (or group mind) that would think this topic through.

In the microseconds after this idea crossed my mind I thought of "rail travel"—of the serenity and luxury of travel by train. However lacking that might be in today's world, rail probably has a remarkable future. I think of the leisure industry, of not simply the wealthy but of many millions of people who will have time on their hands. Of the fact that while we are developing trains that will travel in tubes at 400 mph there is another kind of travel in which families will want to rent cabins on rails where they can be side-tracked to leisure resorts. They do not have to drive and can share time with others. Warren Buffett has invested in rail. Has he seen this? Who knows. But were I to free associate further to this, over time, within a group of fellow dreamers, where would we wind up in a year or two? I assure you: very much further down the line.

17 Morphogenesis

This term, which derives from biology and is now used to discuss the development of a trend in culture, follows on from the LOP. It takes into account that any one line of logic will *disseminate* along the lines envisioned by Freud in his picturing of the unconscious as *ramifying*: of coming together in condensations (joined into a cluster) and then splitting off into many separate dimensions.

So, as I think of rail travel and the leisure industry, I have gone off on a line—no pun intended—of thought in which I imagine designers coming up with demi-containers for families: better than RVs. I think of rail parks, of travel from one side of the continent to another: of going from Santa Barbara, California, to Santiago, Chile with one's family (pets and all), or of going from Istanbul to Delhi, or Moscow to Parma. I am not referring to disparate rail systems, but to using the means we now have to ship containers, now morphed into shipping container homes for leisure. And as I wrote this, the thought of container ships sprang to mind and of families being able to move by sea and by rail for a long and leisurely time. If AI and Androids are to take our place and free us up, might we not have a lot of fun and new adventures that nourish the human mind and spirit?

Were I in a dream group tasked, say, by Marriott Hotels, this idea might have led to the idea of a moving pod, from sea, on rail, or parked in a hotel complex. Another member might have added that with the advent of huge air transports, small container pods (or family pods) could be air lifted across the seas so that families could travel further. Another member might have seen a way for people in business communities to travel and stay for long and meaningful periods of time in parks like "Centerpark" (Belgium/UK) in different countries with families remaining connected to their home base by "hologram community."

How *much* would this cost?

Well, the "average" middle-class family could afford a portable container pod. Given the return of children to families, any family could invest in its pod which would be for a lifetime. Marriott and other companies could compete to offer "transit" locations. A hotel chain, a shipping company, rail links, and aircraft links, all of these points toward a future that is hardly utopian but utterly convenient.

It also takes into account the rise of the "pet" in the lives of human beings: our need for emotional comforters as we head into a rather challenging new world.

In other words, those organizations that understand human needs (I do not refer now to the endless capacity of the unconscious mind for invention, but to the limited capacity of human beings given ordinary emotional requirements) will need to imagine us in highly creative ways.

If you see in the so-called "comfort animal" a precursor of the need in all of us for emotional support as we travel, then you grasp the logic of the present and may be seeing into the future. And in front of you is a huge "pet industry" catering to man's best friend and for all of us.

The world is morphogenic now in ways it never was. *Morphogenic consciousness* is only achieved by multiple lines of thought driven by unconscious perceptions. The more any organization develops these "unconscious eyes" to see into the streams of consciousness generated across countries, realms, and cultures, the more one is morphogenically prepared. This is, specifically, the capacity to see in the early form of a phenomenon a logic of the present that will lead to a complex outcome that will be identified with that object.

Given the vast but acute array of aleatory events meeting the predeterminate elements of a phenomenon, any group must develop a morphogenetic vision. We must imagine the way things will develop.

18 Broader Uses

For obvious reasons, I have focused on the business community. But organizations—and this should include the business world—involved in constructing programs adaptive to the future need to create dream teams that will work in much the way we have been discussing, albeit with a few important differences.

If one were helping a governmental agency in, say, Norway to integrate that nation's unconscious interests in order to attenuate them so that cultural dreaming could be part of small dream teams, the SOOTS would have to be an ongoing designated matrix. This would mean that a team of eight would be reading the same two or three newspapers each day, would be tuned into popular culture—from sports to arts to films and so forth—as the team free associates to cultural dreaming (thus elaborating it and making it more conscious).

The agency—let's imagine it is tasked with thinking through Norway's relation to all significant foreign affairs that impact or are likely to affect Norway—will, every few weeks, pass a specific SOOT to the group. It might simply be the word "Brexit" or it might be a cluster of images, such as "Brexit, South China Seas, Self Drive Cars," which is hardly a logical cluster but therefore more likely to elicit unconscious thinking.

I will have to leave this topic—the wider and varied uses of an RG—as time and our task restricts this, but I wanted the group to get a sense of the differing incarnations of this concept.

In Conclusion

In these two meetings, we have discussed how the formation of a group designed to free associate to a selected object of thought can both elicit and promote unconscious thinking, thus enhancing an organizations perception of reality. By drawing upon both the speed and the complexity of the human brain through the method of free association *and* by forming a group mind to further enhance the reaches of human perception and imagination, organizations moving into the challenges of the twenty-first century can upgrade the human capability.

The seminars have not concentrated on the obstacles to setting up dream teams, nor have they focused on the resistances to this process within the groups themselves. In addition, the wider range and specific uses of this group process are only hinted at.

19 Facing the Future

All generations have faced some form of future, whether it is existential (being in the world) or virtual (as in religious cosmologies). *Looking back,* it is reasonably safe to say that even in tumultuous and frightening times, humans had a sense of space, time, and locality that indicated their journey into some form of future.

Arrogant as it might seem, like many others writing about our times, we face an unprecedented human experience as we confront a future that is not only almost unimaginable, but through our introduction of artificial forms of intelligence, we have mapped out a world in which the human subject would seem to be increasingly displaced by a slick Frankensteinian world in which we may be eliminating ourselves as significant players in controlling the future.

In the past, we have used tools to assist us; indeed, our ability to use tools intelligently and to develop our tool making abilities differentiates Homo sapiens from other species. We could say that by now it is hard wired in us: we are compelled to develop. It is a drive.

That drive to develop has often been worrying, and we all know that Plato and the Athenians fretted over the use of the printed word to convey narrative as they held that insofar as it displaced memory, we outsourced a part of our mind in doing so and diminished ourselves.

By the seventeenth century, when walking became safer in Europe and America, there was a sudden burst of enthusiasm for long-distance walking, which for Rousseau, Wordsworth, Coleridge, Hawthorne, and Melville was essential to the creative process. "I have to walk in order to think," said Rousseau.

But with the advent of trains, automobiles, steamships, and other forms of transport, people stopped walking such long distances, and parks became something like nature reserves in the city, rather like memories of what it once was like to walk and think and get lost in a very particular way.

When Henry Ford discovered that productivity could be vastly increased if his workers did just one thing along an assembly line, the human's relation to his use of tools changed slightly but crucially. Assembly line workers became *part* of the machine, famously identified by Charlie Chaplin in *Modern Times*. Indeed, not only did we become part of the operation, we *identified* with the process of production, ever so slightly subordinating ourselves to the manufacturing process, of which we were now a part.

This change was thinly disguised by an apparent antithesis. In the personas of J.P. Morgan, Rockefeller, Mellon, Ford, and others were modern feudal Lords who seemed in the Victorian and post-Victorian universe to be masters of the universe: hardly the subordinate type!

Even if Hegel had argued long before that the master was a slave to his dominance, this subtle point would be lost on those who amassed vast fortunes and power and became the iconic objects of social worship.

Everyone in the class system wanted the system called hope: to believe that one day they too could be rich and powerful. And today we find slicker and more upscale feudal kings in Buffet, Gates, Jobs, Zuckerman, and so forth. Any of us who have access to a garage and a few friends may proceed—from being an upstart to creating start-ups—that will realize the American dream: now a globalized mental commodity.

We see in Musk and other "future makers" new lords emerging on the horizon, seeming evidence of the flow of human intelligence, power, domination, and regeneration.

Along with these kings are feudal empires that have operated with clear vertical structures: at the top a CEO, next ring the FO and middle managers who are "heads" of fiefdoms, and then descending cascades of lower-level managers. If we add that this structure usually has a Board, that it may have stakeholders or if public will have shareholders, then it mimics something of a democratic kingdom with an electorate and a legislative body to which the CEO is responsible.

Management consultants wonder how they can persuade CEOs or senior management to abandon the more traditional business management models (of a leader who delegates authority to divisions within the company, etc.), but your task is likely to shift in an ironic way. It is unlikely that by 2025 any institution (business, government, NGO, or otherwise) will survive if governed by the hierarchical model, however well managed, however inspired the leadership, and so forth.

Why? Because that system of division of labor will simply not be *fast enough* to gather, process, and implement "breaking news" (a metaphor for the movement of the new). Just as airplanes moved from human-controlled hydraulic systems toward fly-by-wire, companies, countries, (etc.), will be outmoded by *systemic forces*.

Indeed, it is part of my *psychoanalytical argument* that the vertical management structures of the twentieth century are organized forms of denial of the very world they have created. That is, while the laborers on the assembly line *knew* they were part of the movement of the machinery, corporate structures did not know this or rid themselves of such knowledge.

Indeed, while Mary Shelley's *Frankenstein* may be the first omen of the creator being overwhelmed by his creation, by the twentieth century, feature films often portrayed how an inventor or investor was to be overwhelmed by what he had created: the boss becoming the minion or victim.

If we now throw petrol on this slow-burning fire and add the transfer of power from the corporate model to the investment one—from manufacturing to investment—then we create an even more radical split between those seeming financial wizards (like Soros, Buffet, and others) who some how seem to know how to play *market forces* while CEO's and others do not.

But what if the Zuckerbergs and Gates of this world simply got lucky? That it had little to do with their person.

That is, if we see market forces as not human, but as simply forces we have created, our hubris suggests that we humans somehow have a way to manage a system that by its nature cannot be managed!

Let us go further.

Imagine *systemic forces* to be an expansion of *market forces*, but different in that while the Dow/Hang Sing/ or FTSE can measure market forces and while central banks and other institutions can try to influence those forces, when we reach a certain *tipping point*, the global-system will become sets of forces moving at such pace that previously existent managements will not be able to keep up with the forces, much less direct them.

Those of you who are coaches, management consultants, CEOs, or in government—may choose to use psychology (especially psychoanalysis)—to help institutions survive and thrive. But if so, you face a huge first hurdle. Namely, the very architecture of these institutions (and I mean from literally the tall buildings with the CEO at the top to the vertical structure of the organizations internally) are not only ill-suited to govern their creations: they are unwittingly in opposition to it!

Some institutions have at least grasped the manifest content, and from the 1970s onward, we see select de-emphasis of the overbearing power of the CEO or upper management, sometimes profit sharing and even types of decision making shared across the spectrum of employees. We note the Silicon Valley buildings which have scrapped the skyscraper for the more down-to-earth rambling hillside structure that seems to be part of the natural world.

But these decorative changes, although meaningful up to a point have not—it seems to me—derived from an understanding of quite why this apparent horizontalization of power has been necessary. And however much these institutions try to abandon the feudal system, we still find the lords of the manor strutting on the stages of adoring groupies, very smartly dressed and thus seeming to be just like everyone else.

Indeed, note the new costume or vestimentary sign of the self engaged in the future: a man on a stage wearing a knit shirt with no tie, usually in black. Those who address their groups wearing a coat and tie (much less suits) might just as well be on horseback addressing a convention of those investing in self-driving vehicles. We see quite literally those who are in the future and those who are in the past.

I do not want to diminish this *latent* unconscious adaptation to changing circumstances, but *gestural change* is as dangerous as outright opposition to change, as it creates the illusion that modern organizations are . . . well, modern . . . when in fact they are still in resistance to the future which is now rushing into the present like an invading force.

This is not to say that institutions do not create important and profitable objects (they do) nor that they are inflexible, because many appear to be aerobic. But let me lob you a metaphor. Imagine the perfect institution of modern times, the exemplar of progressive management policies and so forth: highly productive. But one day as all go to work, the firm is struck by a virus . . . a real one. They all come down with a deadly virus and within twenty-four hours, everyone is dead.

Imagine that they knew about this virus. It was initially located in a remote part of West Africa. That seemed very far away. Their *sense of impregnability* felt like an automatic *immunization* against the effect of such a virus should it even approach the realm, which I would like to term the *psychic gated community*. The psychic gated community is the natural environment created by the modern institution, which ironically, through its modernity, creates the illusion of safety.

You will sense, I am sure, where we are going now.

Imagine that the virus is a systemic one. A cellular development emerging from the globalized structures that suddenly threatens the very existence of those institutions that have created it.

So *now* here you are, a coach or consultant or in management, witness to an institution's celebrations of the good times, realizing that this celebratory universe is akin to a stunning cruise liner about to be hit by a norovirus that has everyone in all classes—from first to lower berth—sick to death.

You note that the vertical structures of organization (even if disguised by Gucci-type modernity and "natural" habitats) are organizationally ill-suited to the task of dealing with both the *suddenness* and the *vastness* of the systemic impact. Indeed, these institutions are so tied in to the systemic world (after all, i.e., what globalization has accomplished) that they have no idea that they are more vulnerable to sudden annihilation than a rice farmer in China or a dairy farmer in Maine.

There are few certainties in life, and it is dangerous to try to predict the future but if 2008 and Brexit have taught us anything, it is that our world is extremely vulnerable to worldwide systemic collapse.

So, what are *you* supposed to do about this?

The first task, unsurprisingly, is that we have to *think* about this. We need a modern psycho-structural analysis of a social catastrophe that in many ways mirrors the other catastrophes that grasp our attention: climate change and nuclear proliferation.

And what are the common denominators that link these systemic catastrophes?

We discuss this in the next lecture.

20 The Chain of Events

What are the factors that breed systemic collapse?

The first is *time*. We have *very little time* to turn things around before we self-destruct.

Which brings us to the second common denominator. Although Homo sapiens have always been destructive, we are *far* more dangerous to one another than ever before. Social media means that on the political front, if, say, Russia moves troops into Eastern Ukraine, worldwide panic and pressures will lead to lightning-fast reactions from NATO and elsewhere.

However much a Putin (or Merkel, or Hollande) might wish to slow things down, modern leaders are not prepared to deal now with the need for lightning-fast, reasoned judgment. We do not have the political structures in place to function as the political equivalent of a SWAT team: a fast reaction *Peace Force* that will slow events down so that human beings can think, can meet, can talk.

If a Saudi group knocked down an Iranian plane and Iran and Pakistan struck Saudi Arabia with lightning speed, the world does not have structures in place to stop this. If the Chinese navy sinks an American destroyer in the South China Sea and someone like Donald Trump is president, how quickly will this sort of easily imaginable event snap the structures of global organization?

And matters are the same with system market forces. If Brexit were *by chance* to coincide with war in the Middle East, and *by chance* with the collapse of the Brazilian economy leading to anarchy, and naval warfare in the South China Sea (and we could go on) you can see that *the aleatory* becomes a "thing-in-itself."

In the twentieth century, we used to speak of "a chain of events" but now we would have to use a different metaphor: of complexities of overlapping and intersecting chains of events the sum of which overwhelms the geopolitical matrix.

At this point, the old management structures—a president talking to a prime minister, or a Dictator agreeing to talk to an Oligarch, and so on—are moot. Events are moving too fast; indeed, they are moving beyond human control because we have implemented automatic artificial forms of intelligence that will launch weapons with precious little thought.

21 "IT"

In order to think about highly complex matters, I will have to simplify. It would be impossible to find any group of words to identify the pace, disseminative force, and confusional challenge of the IT era, one in which humans have gone from using forms of artificial intelligence to anticipating many of our traditional forms of life being replaced by them.

I shall use the term "globalization" to identify the innumerable matrices that have combined to impose a new world order not just on countries and organizations but on the human mind.

I will begin this discussion with a first step in the act of naming given that part of the challenge will be to find words that we can use to identify the maps of human reality, ones that can apply to the individual and the group.

I will continue to use acronyms that are tweet-like in their brevity and also economical in their ability to signify the idea being employed without slowing down the thinker through the increasingly antiquated use of ordinary sentences.

We continue to use the term "intersecting contextual realities" (ICR) to argue that in order for human beings to perceive, consider, and communicate thoughts about *critical* ICR, we must organize human matrices that can process them. I shall argue that the only tool we have to do this is *the group* rather than the individual and drawing upon the Eastern tradition of thought it is to the group mind that we must turn in order to help us think about ICR.

It will be seen that by "the group" we refer to any number of individuals who *develop* the working group mind, which is no small accomplishment and cannot be haphazard. I will begin with the macro picture before proceeding to single institutions, where most of you work.

We would all agree that given the tensions in Europe, the old "alliance group models" are not only outmoded and inadequate, they are dangerous. NATO is a hazard to everyone's well-being precisely because it automatically requires a thoughtless group response to any threat from another region, especially now, with Russia.

Viewed from the perspective of ICR, NATO is just one contextual reality: its own organization. To be sure, it unites multiple countries (contextual realities) but for one purpose: defense. It does not include Russia in the matrix which is potentially catastrophic.

To fashion a work group able to deal with critical ICRs means that any such group would have to include members from each of the contextual realities. The rotating personnel nature of democracies makes this exceedingly difficult as differing administrations that come into power appoint new personnel and the valuable incremental work of establishing a working group between differing parties is likely to be broken up.

If democracies can be seen *in this respect* to be more dangerous and less efficient than oligarchies or even dictatorships, it might be possible to form dream teams *composed* of *dedicated* representatives of each context. Thus, over time, a group of, say, nine people might meet in person monthly from Sweden, Germany, Russia, the UK, Georgia, and Italy.

The point of selection would have to include quite *different* cultures (and I am sure this list can be improved upon) with each member dedicated to forming a dream team. If any member has as his or her task the political representation of his or her own government, then no RG can be composed. Instead, the group is *just* a think tank. No group will make executive decisions or bind any government to its thought process.

When Gordon Lawrence updated Roheim's concept of cultural dreaming by forming matrices of people from disparate professions, his focus was on the dream. Members reported their dreams, the group thought about the reported dreams, and they went on their way. Lawrence termed this "social dreaming," and dreams were both regarded as forms of social thought, while at the same time, the social dreaming group itself constituted a small society.

The groups I propose would be long-term groups and would be best started by reading—at first—novels (fiction) selected by each member. From there, they could move to poetry and then from there to "pop culture objects": to films, articles, and "cultural nodes" occupying the minds of their society. Most importantly, however, they would watch the media in each country report the news to its population.

You may recall Marshall McLuhan's famous dictum, "the medium is the message," and I will build on this to argue that the media is the message.

That if you wish to get a sense of how a country dreams about the world in which it lives you need to watch the television news, television broadcasts, and then—as importantly—you need to hang out in public locations where people talk about their views.

In time, *trends of thought* (TOT) will emerge and occupy your mind when you think of that particular country and its culture. So, if you are advising any group on its activities in a certain region you can do a TOT test to see if the organization you are advising has or has not done the research necessary to gather the TOT.

I think you will find three types of organizations. The first is one that is multicultural, with employees very much a part of the cultures in which they function. They have a high TOT knowledge base; indeed, to the point that they no longer have to think about TOTs: they have internalized them.

The second is an organization that delegates select individuals to do some research in a country, maybe hands out a small dictionary with select vocabulary for travelers, and gives the organization tourist knowledge of the country. Such an approach will have some TOT knowledge but it will be a form of flirtation with involvement which can be very misleading all around.

The third organization declines any such immersion and takes what we might think of as the Common Ground Approach (CGA), which is predicated on isolating and identifying with those TOTs that are shared amongst the organizations that generate globalization. We might think of this approach in visual terms by imagining any modern city in any country in the world where said city looks like any other city in any other country in the world. That city will also have cars, buses, trams, airports, (etc.) that can be found in any other city in the world.

This matrix does indeed exist, and we will return to it later but for our purposes it has an organized *phobic refusal* of immersion in the TOT of any country. Indeed, it is a form of *mobile xenophobia* that occupies countries by ridding consciousness of the ethnic organization and view of a country—what we might think of as *cultural genocide* and puts in its place the imagery, language, and personnel derived from the CGA.

But let us return to forming groups with a high TOT base who are determined to immerse themselves in the disparate cultures that exist around the world.

The aim is clear: to develop a group's ability to *unconsciously* perceive and communicate culture (and mentality) to one another so that each group eventually forms a collective mind (CM) able to constitute "psychic genera." Psychic genera are epiphanies (or realizations to use Bion) that open up creative new perspectives as a result of unconscious work.

Now, imagine that five such groups of ten people are formed and have worked together for seven years. Three times a year, all five groups (thirty-five people) meet in a retreat simply to discuss their process and the psychological challenges of dealing with ICRs.

(Coaches and consultants should also form their own groups not top-down seminar ones, like mine, but matrices or work groups)

Along the way, they would have formed a knowledge base (KB) with KC and used the art of reverie and daydreaming to draw up (and upon) unconscious creativity in the vital task of processing fast-breaking information that cannot be grasped through consciousness.

Now let us turn to corporations, institutions, and non-governmental organizations where many of you coach, consult, or lead. From the above, you will infer no doubt that I regard traditional vertical structures as defenses against their creation: in this case, a world moving way too fast for such structures to think about what they have created.

You will also infer that CICRs also apply to any medium-sized institution where people function from differing cultures, classes, regions, and so forth. And you will see that I believe it is only by forming dream teams can any institution grasp the impossibly fast-breaking news and information that would overwhelm consciousness. It will be clear that I believe that it is only through *the development and utilization of unconscious perceptions* that we grasp this degree of complexity so that groups are *then* in a position to come to certain forms of conscious decision . . . informed by the work of unconscious processes.

I will return to this topic shortly, but first, we need to confront a well-intentioned but misguided axiom having to do with learning.

22 The Uses of Depression

Now, some of you—if not all—will be scratching your heads and perhaps thinking, "Well, this sounds all well and good, but how the hell am I going to introduce this to my colleagues?" and that is, of course, an imperative question.

Let's see what is on your side should you decide to go down this road. Many of you have written about how anxious people are at the top, how some CEOs are afraid of making decisions for fear of failure, of how the shareholders' or stakeholders' demands are constant and frightful, and how middle management are in constant fear of being sacked because they fail to meet "performance targets."

In other words, your ally here is *anxiety*. It is actually *signal anxiety*, as you know. It is a warning from the unconscious mind to consciousness that something is not working and the self needs to be alerted.

One crucial anxiety is that of *obsolescence*. People are afraid that they will not be able to keep up with new technologies and the challenges they pose. Chasing close behind this is the fear that a new generation of "tekkies" who not only are in full grasp of the new stuff, some have actually invented it!

What is so intriguing about "obsolescence anxiety" is that human beings are mirroring the object world they have created.

You recall the point that workers identified themselves with the manufacturing process. This is the same thing, only one step further along. Feeling obsolete is to identify with the *inevitability of obsolescence* in a culture where the new and improved object will get rid of the old. We begin not only to look at the object world in that way—should I invest in an iPhone or wait for X company to come up with the new form of communication?—but we look upon ourselves and others in the same way.

Should we keep Bloggs in his job much longer, or shouldn't we move and get Joe Smart in here to keep us up to date? Unconsciously, merging a new technological object with a new employee (and getting rid of the obsolete objects) is an *unconscious emotional fact*.

This does not mean that institutions will simply sack people because of that fact, but it does mean that now this latent possibility endemic to any workplace has morphed into a much more powerful phenomenon, which Freud termed "attachment." He did not mean attachment as it is meant today—as in attachment to an other—but that one meaning will be attached to another, thus joining two otherwise different phenomena.

In this case, new technology and new person are attached to one another, creating anxiety in the existing employees and an uneasy feeling in the CEO (and upper management) that they should "rotate people out" and bring in fresh blood, or somehow they are not doing the right thing.

In addition to the anxieties above—and there are others—the people who occupy modern institutions are increasingly *depressed.*

The fear of being obsolete when realized (as one is "let go") turns into depression. How do you help people deal with those innovations that render them obsolete?

Many of you have discussed how, when coaching or consulting you do not feel "fresh," you may feel "marginalized," or "irrelevant." You will know from your studies of projective identification and the countertransference that you are holding those feelings for the very people whom you coach, consult, or organize. Given the systemic issues I will return to, no one will be feeling fresh, all will feel marginalized and irrelevant.

Your task will be to bring to the attention of your client that these feelings of yours are referred to you and the way you articulate *your* human dilemma will help them find words (thus far impermissible) for their own depressions.

Here, we need to draw upon the *history* of corporate, institutional, and governmental structures in dealing with depression. Traditionally, this is dealt with by firing the CEO or the chair of the Institute. Democracies have a certain unconscious intelligence insofar as mental depressions are averted through elimination of "old and failed thinking" by bringing in a new person. A task for the future of those in consultancy will be to draw upon *this common structure* (replacement is rejuvenating) to indicate that although this may create a temporary euphoria the evasion of depression through manic replacements dooms any group to eventual failure.

But what you might well ask is *the use* of enduring depression when you can energize your client, a company, institution, or country through new blood?

Because these mental depressions are actually invaluable forms of thinking, when if tolerated, are implicit recognitions that ordinary human beings are failing. But what if recognition of failure is vital to the task of *reflection* and indeed the *eventual* accumulation of wisdom?

Depression—especially bipolarity—is the leading mental health problem worldwide. Yet what if this ailment, which we medicate in order to get us back into more functional beings, could become a transition to a wiser and eventually more astute human being, humane society, and yes, more productive company or country? Indeed, what if depression is actually essential to survival over the long run as it slows selves and institutions down, which if undertaken collectively (i.e., regarded worldwide as a rather important step) could slow up manic technologization?

While it is of course true that paralyzing anxiety or depression stops selves from thinking, much less from being creative, both emotions are regular features of human beings and each serves important psychic, relational, social, and creative functions.

For example, the Ukrainian nationalism that led to the "revolution" that ousted Porochenko was heralded by the media as an act of freedom and evidence of the move toward democracy in that country. Astute politicians in Europe, however, were anxious. It was not as virtuous a movement as it made out and although the ousted Porochenko was corrupt, politicians knew that Ukrainian calls to become part of the European Community would, of course, raise anxiety in Russia.

The speed of events and the refusal to publicly consider—much less discuss with Russia—the understandable concerns on the part of Russians that such nationalism was an aggressive threat to their integrity, led to many diplomats and internationalists feeling depressed over the oversimplification of complex matters.

Those feelings on the part of Western leaders—of anxiety and of depressive concerns—had they been communicated to Putin and the Russians, could have developed international empathy instead of triumphalism. This is not a matter of any Western government telling the Ukranians that they had to remain in the Russian orbit—that would be absurd and almost equally confusing to the Russians—but failure to indicate an empathic identification of how this looked through Russian eyes transformed that situation into violent conflict and very possibly into a renewal of the cold war.

23 Daydreaming

Imagine you are a consultant to what I will term "Park With Us," a large corporation that has invested in car parks around the world. You have, of course, costed into your plans the tradition of people getting to the venue (airport, concert hall, sports stadium) by taxi or rail but the statistics provided rock solid evidence that people preferred to drive themselves to these venues and this was a solid investment.

Then along comes Uber. Suddenly, people who would not take a taxi because it was too expensive and also unpredictable—one was never sure that taxis would be around when needed—turned to this new app that showed them, repeatedly, that they could be dropped off and need not drive to the venue.

Ripples of anxiety course through the corporation. You are in the midst of the Uber problem when all of a sudden, rather out of the blue, Google announces the startlingly imminent arrival of the self-driving car. All of you read an article in the newspaper that speculates that self-driving cars will, of course, return to the owner's home rather than park and wait. And as if to make matters even worse, articles appear claiming that self-driving cars will allow passengers to make love while heading from point A to B, giving sexual incentive to the self-driving: the seeming death knell of car parks.

Wherever you coach or work, organizations have to be ready for this kind of sudden and fast change.

The traditional approach to a problem like this would be to summon a meeting of departmental heads, to create a task force that would work on this problem, to delegate to members of the team differing sub-tasks, and to set performance standards before the next meeting, and the next, and the next. Staff might be informed that they would have to work long hours, forgo vacations, and so forth. The Board of Directors of "Park With Us" has set a deadline for a response to this challenge, set for two months before the annual shareholders meeting which is dreaded as your stock has dropped 15 percent since news of the self drive, and this is a drop on the part of smart investors who are getting out before the penny drops.

The CEO might give a Henry V speech to the team before shouting at them to jump over the walls to solve this problem, but if so, this is not a good idea. Nor are targets or performance expectations.

You will appreciate that I am arguing for a functioning group mind to be present and ready to deal with all challenges. A reactive task force to such an issue might fire off some immediate neural shots in the dark, but this is the least likely way to be productive.

The solution is definitely counterintuitive. It would be for a heterogeneous group of the corporation (let's say fifteen people, with two middle executives, a person in research, and others way down the food chain, right to one member who man's a cash kiosk at a local car park. They know each other, have been to one another's homes for Saturday visits when they chill out and cook together.)

They will constitute a reverie work group (RG), which is an offshoot of the work group discussed above. You may recall D. W. Winnicott's concept of "the period of hesitation" which is crucial to his observation of how infants "use the object." He would sit across the end of a table with the infant on the mother's lap and talk with the mother, taking note of the infant now and then. When he felt the moment was right, he would take a spatula (wooden tongue depressor that doctors use all the time to examine your tongue or throat) and put it on the table in full view, and reach, of the infant. He noticed that almost always as soon as the infant saw the object they would *turn away* and look elsewhere. After some moments they would then turn and look very directly at the object, and I am told, would often be drooling with salivary anticipation that they might be able to get hold of that object and put it in their mouth.

The paradox is clear. For an infant to use an object, you cannot hand it to him directly as he will turn away and lose interest, or cry. But if he has time to imagine it—by turning away—then it becomes an object of desire and he can then use it.

Let's move forward to recent scientific studies of daydreaming: the modern form of play and creativity in everyday life. It is important that we take the time to provide this evidence because *if* you are to propose RGs to your clients, then a "faith based" proposal will not be a bread-breaking moment. On the other hand, if you provide the increasingly impressive research studies—that demonstrate how a wandering (or day dreaming) mind is more productive than a task-oriented and concentrated mind, you are likely to get to the dining table.

Gilbert and Killingsworth of Harvard found that people's minds wander forty-seven percent of waking time.[1] Ironically, these times are our most productive mental moments. We are actually thinking . . . a lot. To add to the irony, our minds are more likely to wander when we are *bored* which means that whatever task we have been handed, our minds have plenty of left-over capacity that appears to go unused but in fact is actually thinking outside the bounds of conventional focusing, through the day dream.

Benjamin Baird and Jonathan Schooler of UCSB ran an experiment in which they asked 145 undergraduates to perform identical tasks. They were given a list of items and asked to itemize their uses. The items were ordinary objects—toothpicks, bricks, and clothes hangers.

The students were divided into "four different conditions," writes Lehrer. In three of the conditions the students were given a twelve-minute break during which they resided either in "a quiet room, performing a difficult short-term memory task, or doing something so boring that it would elicit mind-wandering." In another condition all participants were given no break at all. In a final control, all participants were given a new set of creative tests as well as a repeat presentation of the "unusual-use tasks" they had worked on minutes before.

When given the new items to think about, all the groups performed the same. But when asked to think again about the items to be used, the group that was placed in a boring space outperformed the other groups. In fact, on repeats of this paradigm, the group allowed to be bored came up with forty-one percent more possibilities than students in the other groups. Schooler concluded that the twelve minutes of daydreaming allowed the students to access their unconscious minds. Indeed, boredom was "incubation"—time in which the mind could access much deeper levels of thought than would ordinarily be the case.

In a startling study of dreaming and creativity, Ullrich Wagner and Jan Born (in the Lehrer article) published in *Nature* in 2004, gave students a tedious task of transforming a long list of number strings into a shorter list. Wagner and Born had designed the task so that there was a shortcut to solving this task if people saw it, but less than twenty percent did so, even though the students were allowed hours to work on the task. Then Wagner and Born changed the study by creating a nap time in which the group was able to gain REM sleep, after which sixty percent of the students discovered the shortcut.

Time does not permit a history of this interesting topic, but scores of other research studies—in many different locations—come up with the same conclusion.

A wandering mind is a creative one.

There are many conclusions one can draw from these studies. It is easy enough to discern that employees who are in a room with a manager who wants to see alert and concentrated faces—"look sharp there Briggs!"—is actually a psychological block to increased creative thinking. So too would a work group headed up by an anxious CEO find it hard to come up with new ideas if it met for an hour or so in which people were meant to "brain storm." "Are we boring you Briggs?" a CEO might say to a colleague who is caught looking out the window. The CEO, just like the classroom school teacher, has mistakenly (although understandably) taken the daydreaming moment to be bunking off and by honing in with his razor-sharp intelligence, the leader is actually preventing the group from thinking.

Now, you are a consultant to "Park With Us" or a coach to the CEO, and the organization wants results. *If* you have worked with them long enough to form reverie groups then the participants can meet, chill out, and take their minds off work and presumed tasks. They have managed to do this. When in a moment's boredom, while riding the elevator, or sitting in traffic, one member of the group's mind wanders (as will they all be) he or she may suddenly have a solution to the dilemma facing the company. At this point, he calls up the team and they chat on the line and *subject* the inspiration to a free associative process, making one person's inspiration the group's object of thought.

But what if the idea dies in the group talk?

It has to be *no big deal*. Everyone must be free to be quite wrong or even crazy in his or her thinking.

When together—just chilling—the RG is open for anyone to present a dream. Here, I refer to Lawrence's paradigm of social dreaming, how the dream picks up latent issues in the culture and thinks about them. Given the fact that the unconscious naturally concentrates on high value matters—again what Freud termed objects of "high psychic value"—a reverie group's dreams will always be forms of thought *about* the elements of life in the group. If you are the consultant or the coach then you could be "the host" to the RG but that simply means you host the meetings, begin and end them, and stay out of the way.

But what about the attention being focused on the RG by the CEO, management, shareholders, parking lot attendants, and the like?

The secret is that *they are* a secret.

The CEO and a few others who have taken a solemn vow to leave them alone have created—to use Winnicott—a "potential space" and know that the RG has to be forgotten about. This does not mean that the CEO and others could not form their own focus group, isolating tasks and going through the traditional problem-solving steps. Why not? Importantly, it provides valued cover for the RG so that it can get on with its paradoxical task unintruded upon by the others.

At the end of the day, the proof will be in the pudding. If you are proposing this to the CEO it is simple enough to say "let's let the results speak for themselves" and off the productivity lines of human thought it will become startlingly clear which group is more productive: the task group or the reverie group.

What does this have to do with facing the future?

As discussed, we live in a fast-moving global world that cannot be apprehended by consciousness but is available for unconscious thinking, especially in the dream or the daydream. The RG maximizes the potential for unconscious reception of the complexities of the day and also perceives the future, a well-known—indeed ancient fact—that dreams were prophetic. What the Sumerians and others realized was that dreams not only perceive existent reality, they use that to forecast the future, to involve the self in a future that has used the wisdom of the past to form a matrix for perception.

While anxiety and depression are important affects that register our emotional involvement in existential realities—and are of value—the RG *is a pleasure* and like the dream draws on the epistemophilic drive and the life instinct that enjoys discovery and the combinatory play of unconscious processes. Put differently, we enjoy playing with reality, a phrase made famous by D. W. Winnicott.

Whether consulting with a corporation, a university, an NGO, or a government, if we utilize the 100 billion or so brain cells with which we are endowed, and if we let the brain authorize our minds to roam according to its pleasures then even the challenge of the horrific is a novel exercise for unconscious work. After all, it is just a dream: isn't it?

24 The Production of Meaning

Before concluding today, we need to confront a resistance to change. It is a well-intentioned one; indeed, it is hiding in plain sight as this is a most ironic resistance indeed. Across the organizational and professional worlds you will be well aware of what we can broadly class as "continued professional development": seminars given by numerous leaders in their fields that will improve organizational skills and productivity. It hardly escapes our notice that I would fall into this genre.

And although *some* seminars and thinkers do help groups to approach their task with new visions that may become transformative, unfortunately we face a vast new industry of "commodified knowledge." Entire organizations have sprung up around the globe with the sole purpose of training and certifying people to give workshops and seminars that update professionals on the latest forms of knowledge that—we are told—are essential to updating us as we move along the education highway.

Following along the road of ordinary profit, the tens of thousands of people in the commodified industry have, of course, lobbied governments (local, regional, national) and professional regulatory agencies to make CPD's (or "continuing professional development") credits mandatory in many cases. And who will do the teaching to supply the mandated to earn the annual required credits? If you have guessed that it is the commodified knowledge industry you would not be wrong and who can blame them for cashing in on a demand that they have lobbied to become mandatory?

In my antiquated profession—mental health—we now have annual CPD requirements that also target special areas where we must update our practice with certified expertise in specific areas, such as child abuse. Perfectly legitimate areas of concern become economically profitable if we can turn an ethical concern into a profit-making industry.

Now to our point.

The problem with so-called experts providing the latest "cutting edge" views is that they sustain the "top-down" view of the acquisition of knowledge and the development of "K" (to remind us, this is Bion's term for knowledge. –K is the presumed acquisition of knowledge or its communication that *actually* subtracts from the knowledge function or its base). The top-down approach sustains not simply an archaic form of learning but one which is now counterproductive. Indeed, many of these courses and seminars are the educational equivalent of snake-oil salespeople, selling –K to the clients. By this we mean that instead of promoting knowledge such commodified transmissions actually detract from knowledge, emptying the minds of the clients, the organizations, and the professions.

You will appreciate that by forming work groups from *within* organizations, by understanding the nature of unconscious perception, and the learning capital to be gained through submersion in culture, such working groups will *produce meaning*. The production of meaning is, arguably, our most important form of production. It *will* be profitable but not at the expense of people. It will actually use our neurological banks, our individual and collective minds to *grasp reality, generate visions, and develop new forms of organization essential to our survival.*

25 The Pool of Knowledge and the Future

To remind us, our focus is on *the future* and in particular *facing the unknown.* While we would all agree there is an *absolute unknown*, in that there are certain events or things which we could not possibly imagine now, the more probable unknown is that which is unknown *to consciousness.*

You will grasp from my writings and yesterday's lecture that I believe there is a lot that we know unconsciously and more to the point, that unconscious processes can and do perceive the future. From the words of prophets, to the forecasts of the dream, from the oracles of Delphi, to the cosmologies of the future proposed by the religions, from the novels about the future, to films that take us into the many differing versions of the future, we have always been thinking about it.

However, future thinking—let's use the modern term for it "futurology"—is the object of considerable contempt. This may be deservedly so if anyone's "forecast" (fore-cast) is meant to be taken as definitive. And it may well be that however beautiful some of the religions are in constructing a sublime future for us, the "end of the world predictions" that have never come true have perhaps turned us off from forecasting and from belief in futurology.

Another dimension is that our mortality no doubt plays a role in our disinclination to become futurologists. As we die all too soon, why invest in thinking about the future, most of which we will not be around to see?

Indeed, mortality breeds a certain life span myopia that rigorously focuses on the present or the very near and palpable future which we think we can control. Further, our failure to learn from clear patterns in the past that should be relatively fair predictors of the TF (economic, political, ecological) may not only be due to our narcissism, greed, or whatnot, but to a more universal and shared human dimension: to our life span myopia.

Life span myopia is a collective character disorder in which *unconsciously* we assume we are *the only generation.* Mortality does not simply suggest that the world ends when we die, but that before we existed there was no world.

Thought about this way, it is easy to see that although we can and do study history (of economics, politics, ecology, etc.), we actually do not see the relevance to ourselves of much of this. Viewing this only as a form of narcissism misses the mark, in my view, if I am right that this is a universal human characteristic.

Indeed, this myopia may have been phylogenetically essential. Early Homo sapiens may have had to live within the notion that each generation had to invent itself in order to survive. Perhaps there could be no sense of the past and no need for history, much less a forecast of the future, because we had to think here and now about how to survive.

If this wereso, it would have been true for several hundred thousand years and become part of our neural organization. Namely, we may still not have developed a part of the brain—and thus of its different but vital offshoot, the mind—that can really imagine a LTF.

At the very best, we seem inclined to *worry on behalf of our children* who have to face a future that we may have handed to them, but however empathic this may seem, it is an odd form of abandonment. We presume—falsely—that while we failed to manage the future, maybe their youth and inventiveness will come up with something radically transformational.

i. Psychic Genera

You may recall from yesterday's lecture that I placed considerable focus on the value of unconscious thinking. I discussed how the formation of reverie work groups could *heighten unconsciousness* in order that *psychic genera* be formed that would burst into consciousness as *forms* of inspiration. A couple of people sitting around in a garage mulling things over—long periods of silence or the sort of talk that is akin to free association—is suddenly jolted when one of them jumps up and says "wait a minute. What if . . ." and suddenly an idea that has arisen out of this RG and the matrix of the group unconscious is born.

That is a psychic genera.

So, let us take this sample from the known to help us with the presumed unknown. All of you coaching, consulting, or managing face aspects of your clients' or organizations' anxieties about the future. There is nothing new about that, but as discussed yesterday, the pace of the future (I have said it is *invading* the present) makes it urgent to develop the capacity to think about, forecast, and engage the future: near (NF: now to 5 years), long term (LTF: 5–50 years), and very long term (VLTF: 50–200) and extremely long term (ELTF: 200—000). What is the point of defining these epochs?

Mental organization.

Unconscious receiving areas.

If we train our conscious minds to fashion epochs like this *and name them,* then our unconscious minds (remember, our way of thinking thousands of thoughts from moment to moment) will meet the requests of consciousness.

Naming also puts thoughts into the verbal lexicon and thus gives them not only a linguistic space but, more importantly the terms instantiate in the symbolic order (c.f. Lacan) concepts that can then be verbally exchanged. This capacity for verbal exchange, or verbal currency (VC), is crucial to the transmission of KC, a concept that has fortunately taken hold in recent decades.

Okay, let us now return to thinking about the future.

ii. The pool of ideas

Imagine we have formed reverie work groups that utilize unconscious thinking and facilitate the creation of psychic genera. We now go a step further. Such groups are *themselves* part of an *evolutionary psychology* vital to our survival in facing the future. However important individual genera might be, they are far less significant—in the LTF—than the "pool of ideas" that each group forms.

Let's put this into verbal form: not the pool of ideas, but the pooling of ideas, that result in a pool of ideas. Even seemingly bad ideas in the pool may turn out much later to be astute. The point, however, is that groups are now forming not simply stand-alone ideas, not just developing a utilitarian science of subjectivity, but each group—and their interconnection with other groups—is forming the *future pool* (FP).

Imagine that an enlightened corporation or government has formed reverie groups that use dynamic consciousness to imagine the future. They create hundreds, indeed thousands, of ideas that constitute the pool of ideas. They also develop *the skill of "pooling,"* which can only take place in a positive and receptive group atmosphere that does not demonstrate contempt toward this form of thinking.

In time, a pool of ideas will be formed, and as events in the real world impact the community (remember, the future is invading the present), certain ideas within the pool will "light up." In other words, we will already have thought about the future and in some ways figured it out, but until events light up a matrix within the pool then we cannot move them into *heightened consciousness.*

Let us remember that if we look back almost all of the creations of the future were imagined long, long before they arrived. Whether it is the wheel, gun powder for defense, or whatnot, individual thinkers and civilizations have thought about and created objects in their own time that, *in the future,* will be rediscovered.

It is upon this rediscovery that we get a creative epiphany. It will be out of the pool of ideas, more actively generated by reverie work groups in our time, that as the future knocks on our doors of perception, we will be able to respond with previously thought visions of what to do.

To conclude this segment of our process, the FP is an unconscious matrix developed and utilized by the group mind. It *becomes,* in time, an active part of mental life to the point of its being structuralized.

iii. The group mind

The best example I know of to point to the structurization of the group mind is to point to Confucius and the *Analects*. Confucius lived from 551 to 479 BCE, and we are meant to believe that he wrote some of the aphorisms of the Analects. But like Lao Tsu, Confucius is referred to as *Confucius* because the *Analects* are not the work of one person, but of groups of Chinese scholars and thinkers *over centuries.*

In *China on the Mind,* I argued that the Chinese, for various reasons, had a preconception of the challenges of mass society and through the development of a CM were preparing themselves for that future.

Unfortunately, that incredibly creative collective group process was scuttled with the cult of personality forming around Mao, even though ironically, Mao was a leader of the collective movement termed communism. Therein lies the gruesome paradox. No communist movement could ever have a leader! The mere idea of a leader of a communist country is a contradiction.

Lenin and others tried to confront that malignant contradiction, imagining a time when society would be leaderless, with each soviet (small community group) using the group mind to maximize productivity. The Kibbutzim in Israel came a lot closer to constructing creative group life, and to be historically fair, even though Russia, China, and Israel failed to follow the logic of the group these were important historical steps in the right direction.

What is the solution to the problem posed by a group's turn toward a leader?

As mentioned a moment ago, it is mental structurization. Chinese society has structuralized the axioms indigenous to the group mind. They share a phenomenal group unconscious—or rather, they have developed the capacity to think as a group.

On a smaller and more relevant scale, however, if we look into the future, we will have to form small RGs to slowly structuralize the process so that it will become part of the collective unconscious and finally part of the way we go about thinking about things. I understand that this may seem to be a tall order, but great accomplishments—like great rivers—start way upstream from a source that seems absolutely inconsequential.

So, let's return to praxis.

iv. "Praxis"

What do you do with these considerations for your company or institution?

I am sure you have been imagining how your colleagues back home will roll their eyes to the ceiling (or heavens) were you to even try to present some of these ideas. Psychoanalysts terms this resistance, as you know, and it is to be taken seriously.

What Freud termed the death instinct is perhaps the most powerful resistance there is, although it often does not come to the mind of analysts as a resistance. In short, the death instinct is a de-cathexis (withdrawal of interest in) the outside world and a turning in upon the self to the point of thoughtlessness and then non-existence. Its handmaidens are "denial," "dissociation," "reaction formation," "mania," and "obsessive-compulsive" circularity amongst others. Okay, but still, *how* do you break through this stuff?

We have to expand Freud's thinking on the death instinct a bit. We add "the mortality complex," which is any self's withdrawal from investment in life after the point that the self realizes it will be extinguished. Infants and toddlers—who do not usually know about death yet—need the smiling mother and family to present novel objects that invite endless surprise and curiosity and aid and abet the life instincts. Corporations, start-ups, and many institutions fall within this early infantile realm as they love to be presented with *anything new*! Newness is life, it would seem. Newness and surprise are endlessly promising.

Then time passes.

The latency-age child realizes that people die and this is disturbing. He wants to talk about it but is usually told not to worry and that it is so far away from him that death might as well be on the planet Pluto, light years away. And institutions go through their own latency phase we might say in which they too have a disturbing inkling that they might go under, but . . . what the heck, this is way too far into the future to think about.

Adolescence is a bio-psychological surge that is so tumultuous—full of passions that go up and down—that death seems Shakespearean: the *petite mort* of orgasm. And we can add that institutions are easily medicated against knowledge of the mortality complex by intoxicating successes, such as happens at Apple, Google, or you name it.

The lifespan from this point on, however, is *staged* in such a way that each ten-year span brings selves into increasingly complex relations to their mortality: far too complex to discuss here. At some point, the realization of mortality becomes complex because we are not deft at dealing with our mortality: hence the term "complex." Again, way too complicated to discuss now. But the mortality complex looked at now from the point of view of your praxis is something that all of you can address with your clients.

Recall the "new blood" regeneration we discussed yesterday and the idea that any organization can survive if it brings in youth. This stress bears on all in the workplace, and even though top-level management can escape and go elsewhere (we might call this the "heaven fantasy" as they think they are always going to climb the stairway to immortality), those who are a stable part of the organization will be caught up in potential premature rigor mortis which is akin to death preparation.

This may sound fanciful—that managers and others might be practicing death—but we need not read Melville's *Moby Dick* where Queequeg gets in and out of his coffin day after day—practicing death—to know that our mortality complex might lead us into this direction.

But again, praxis.

Whatever do you say?

Let's imagine this as a dialogue between you and your client. She or he may be the CEO, middle management, a cabinet minister, or whoever.

Client: So, what's on the agenda for today?

You: How about death?

Client: Sorry?

You: Death.

Client: What the hell? Are you *kidding*?

You: Well, we may laugh about this—for sure—but no, I'm serious if you are okay with it. We can always talk about it later.

Client: Look, I like you, but what the heck does this to do with our (corporation, institution, government, etc).

You: A lot, actually.

Client: Okay, like what?

You: Our knowledge of our deaths keeps us short-sighted.

Client: Short-sighted?

You: Yes, because we know we are going to die, even though we try to come up with novel ideas and new inventions, we are—or many are—simultaneously dealing with restrictions in our thinking and envisioning because of this limitation.

Client: How does it limit us?

You: We try to believe our corporation (or institution, nation, etc.) will be around endlessly, but we see other companies fail, (etc.) and we know we shall all perish. So, without even knowing it—although we try to deny this by bringing in new people and providing ourselves with the illusion of immortality—we are fighting a paralyzing anxiety, but it is not easy to talk about.

Client: Yes, but how does it limit us?

You: If we know we will die eventually, we just give up thinking creatively long term and resort to the "hope complex" in which we wish our successors the best of luck.

Client: And so how can we use this presumed knowledge? What good does it do us?

You: Well, actually, we are mortal but ideas are not. And while it is impossible for us to know whether or for how long our company or government will exist, we can begin to create groups that will create longer futures for ourselves.

Client: Longer futures?

You: Yes, we actually can form groups right now that, in a few years' time, will be able to see into the future, create new possibilities, and give birth to forms that might indeed carry us along for a very long time.

Client: Well, surely you don't mean that; therefore, we get to think we will all be immortal by proxy!

You: No, absolutely not. But by creating *our relation to the future after our deaths,* we overcome the paralysis of the mortality complex.

Client: You mean, even though we are not immortal, we can mitigate the paralyzing effects of the mortality complex *because* we can have a relation to the future?

You: Yes. A lot of scientists will not live to see if their project will prove itself or not—they know this—but they do have a vision of the future, and their accomplishment is rather like a strong beacon that casts a light that they follow, even though they know they will not see the product upon which it casts its light in the future.

Client: Um . . . well. But surely you don't expect me or anyone to go out to our colleagues and try to sell them on this idea, do you?

You: No, not directly. But if we form reverie groups that accomplish what I have just been discussing, we won't have to make this conscious. It will just "click in" with their unconscious life as they will become part of it.

Client: Well, we will have to give this a hell of a lot of thought. We need to get some people together to really think this through.

You: I think you should sleep on it. Just see what comes up. That's part of the process, and if you just trust this idea for a while, let's see how it settles with you.

v. Logic of the present

Now you will see the point of this somewhat stilted dialogue if we recognize that the opening move is to get the client to engage in "negative capability" (willing suspension of disbelief) so that you then can host the first RG. Your skill will be in your selection of the members of the group and in the months and possibly years to come in protecting them from the expectation that they will be productive. They will be, and their "products" of imagination can be delivered but you will have a big task ahead as you protect them from *hypertrophied consciousness:* that is, the heightened and anxious consciousness of management as they seek to push that group to become even more productive.

In time, your RGs will start to produce ideas and the fFP will be formed. From this matrix emerges *the logic of the present* which is actually an unconscious reading from the present of which roads to build into the future.

Think of "Park With Us" and the analysis of the logic of the present and how its RG might have produced interesting pathways derived from that logic. For example, driving across the United States this year, I noticed that only a few petrol stations had set up Tesla charge sites for electric cars and also noticed that only a few motels had the same. Looking on the web sites of motels and hotels *none* advertised parking slots for electric cars even though they are now able to drive longer distances.

Even if it is two to three years before we get a car that can do 400–500 miles a day, these companies are *behind the times* and supply prima facie evidence of a failure in perceiving the logic of the present. This is not simply a question of eventually "catching up" because right now even if those few sites that have Tesla sites unfilled and used are actually "ahead of the game" and are advertising themselves as "with it," the sort of place one would want to stay or use—because that sort of physical evidence of prescience (that evokes confidence and trust in the consumer) is not evident. That is, innovation here is not simply a matter of physical productivity but of psychological production.

What is being produced?

vi. Trust futures

Let's term such physical products "trust futures." A trust future is any object that builds trust in the future of its use. The more a company develops trust futures, the more it hedges against inevitable losses in the future because in the psyche of the consumer there has been a bank of TF's built up over the future, so like Toyota or Volkswagen which had disastrous faults in vehicles in 2015—that temporarily resulted in cut back in sales—they have sufficient trust futures so that they will not lose so many consumers in the long run.

Let us now turn our focus from long-term planning to something quite different. Let's consider how "we" deal with unexpected, violently sudden, ramifying catastrophes that could bury our institutions. If we know anything about the past we understand that Homo sapiens need to create predictables.

Think of how religious rituals in churches create highly predictable ceremonies that help us through the unpredictable.

We have evolved—rather on the side—idioms of organization from which we can learn and use in facing the unpredictable. Let's term this idiom the "fast reaction team," derived from SWAT teams (part of "early responders"), to emergency services of all sorts.

The structure and mentality of these groups are about as far away from market forces as one can get because they are predicated upon an interesting assumption: that is, even in a catastrophic situation if we have "pre-existent response structures" (PERS) in place then we have groups that *instinctively and immediately* know what to do.

We do not have time to discuss how any corporation, institution, or government would form its own PERS—I leave this to your imagination—but it will certainly have benefited from a very different organizational group (the FP we have discussed), even if the PERS will no doubt have very different personnel. From a psychoanalytical perspective the PERS is equivalent to "ego organization" and to the "strengthening of the ego" but in the Freudian-western sense of this term, as that mental agency that is intelligently adaptive to changes in reality: internal and external.

But a PERS that is set up to free hostages or put out fires is one thing, while its equivalent in a business, institution, or government that deals internationally is another. And we note that there are ad hoc equivalents of sorts in these institutions, but not adequately thought through due to the inherent narcissism of tradition and the disinclination to embrace the new that is a feature of the death instinct. So, I do not underestimate the problems of forming PERS even though they are literally vital to our survival.

However, it is noteworthy that most institutions do not have PERS. And if they are constructed ad hoc, they can do more damage than good.

In the global economy and international relations, any PERS will develop expertise in relation to its foreseeable tasks which will have been set up through the FP.

(FPs develop expertise).

vii. Catastrophic failure

Let me give an example of a catastrophic failure of expertise. When the United States removed Saddam Hussein from power, there were few, if any, Middle Eastern scholars—who knew the history of that region—involved in the deliberations. Seasoned diplomats and internationalists were marginalized.

It was utterly predictable that the logic of removing Saddam Hussein from power would create a power vacuum, would increase the scope of Shia Muslim interests in the region, alienate the Sunnis, and be contrary to all interests worldwide.

The consequence of this disastrous failure of judgment is still being felt—through the understandable and predictable rise of ISIS—and yet to this day "world leaders" duck the responsibility of stating the obvious. George W. Bush looking back on his disastrous imaginary-driven venture has said "history will be the judge," meaning he will be long dead and bears no actual responsibility.

There are other catastrophic failures that continue to foster worldwide disorder. Ask almost any Middle East historian, or any Muslim family in that region (or indeed worldwide) what issue they believe began to radicalize members of their faith. If you ask the adolescents or even those up to their mid-twenties in that community *they will not know* because the origins of the conflict *have been structuralized:* that is, they now constitute the axioms of people in that religion.

But the parents do know. It was—and up to a point still is—the failure to resolve the Israeli-Palestinian conflict that built up over decades malignant processes that led an otherwise peaceful community to fragment.

All Muslims were disturbed by the Shatila massacre in 1982, and while some in the West found it distressing, the West's decision to ignore the profound shock and trauma to the Muslim world of that action created a fissure between that region and the rest of the world that puts us in a near-catastrophic position.

I use this example because everyone in this room will know of it—even if some or many will disagree with my analysis—in order to make a simple point relevant to corporate or institutional operations around the world. There is no substitute for developing experts in the cultures within which you operate.

Indeed, to go further, each such institution needs *internationalists,* by which I mean not only someone who devotes his or her time to the study of cultures but who maps out and follows international relations. If your corporation produces high-grade plastic-compound pipes for moving water or for irrigation and your company is in Israel you will want to think very carefully about which countries (or regions) in which to invest. Bearing in mind that *hypnotic hype* (HH)—the kind that got the United States to invade Iraq—will inevitably show up to urge you to invest in any sort of place, there is no substitution for deep cultural knowledge (DCK) of any place of investment.

So, while BRIC was a good idea, of the countries involved, historical and cultural analysis would indicate that India is a good bet for investment but Brazil is not. Yet, Brazil has been a much better self-advertiser of its future potential than India has. Its HH factor is very high and India's is very low. It would take an institution with DCK to know this difference and to figure that for all kinds of reasons (that could be articulated), India is a better bet for long-term investment than Brazil.

What does this have to do with catastrophes and the PERS?

International development and investment demand that any institution operating abroad understand that knowledge of a culture is the equivalent of knowledge of how to put out a fire, or respond to an earthquake, or the like. Companies can globalize but globalization does not mean that one is worldly.

The difference is crucial.

Worldliness, here, I will take to be knowledge of the countries and cultures existing across the planet. Globalization, I shall take to be an economic term that identifies capital and technical investment across the planet. At the moment, we are globalized, but unfortunately, this process has exceeded worldliness, and the disparity between the two is as devastating in its potential as is the disparity between the 99 percent and the 1 percent.

Globalization is ICR but only at an economic-technological level, part of the ancient history of trade relations. A question you raised in your emails was what do you do if, say, your company is based in Ireland and you outsource production of part of your product to Bulgaria where you find that they think and behave in such a different way that you now find yourselves in a pickle. Things are not working out.

You are a coach or a consultant.

What can you do to help?

viii. Worldliness

You will grasp from the last ten minutes that the first thing to do would be to increase your "worldliness" by studying the history, literature, music—the culture—of Bulgaria. But... Important as that is, you will have to do something else, and it is not natural. You will have to send all strata of your staff—from senior to middle to worker level—to Bulgaria. Not to live in hotels or the like. You will have to live in the homes of Bulgarian families for at least several weeks *before* you decide whether this is or is not the place to outsource.

If you meet in hotels or conference centers, you might as well save yourselves the time and abandon the effort.

Why should something so evidently simple, such as asking members of staff to spend two weeks (or more) living in Bulgarian families, be so off the map?

Why would it inevitably build resistance? Because to live within the culture—in homes—is to insist that one opens the unconscious mind to receive an alien culture. It is to cultivate *intimate knowledge* (IK) as opposed to *distant knowledge* (DK). If you are a consultant studying why any corporation or institution is not doing so well in any country one of the first questions to ask is where they meet. If the answer is in a hotel you know right away that your consultee is *resistant* to the very thing that he or she aspires to.

To live within a family is, of course, to enter the realms of ordinary cultural clash (OCC), and you and your hosts will have to endure this. You can read about cultural traits and this helps, but if you are going to put serious money into a foreign venture, you have to be prepared to live there, and to experience *firsthand* what it means to think and behave Bulgarian.

I learned this when I was twelve. My father was vice president of the Birtcher Corporation, a leading innovator in medical equipment in the mid-twentieth century. He was French and lived in Paris until he was ten but his stepfather, who was CEO of a large international grain firm moved them all to Buenos Aires, so he learned the language and culture of Argentina and South America.

As VP, he was in charge of international sales and the company was searching to expand into the Japanese market. He did something very clever. He invited a young and highly gifted senior-level figure in a Japanese firm (that was interested in Birtcher products) to come and live with us for three months. It was an amazing and transformative experience for all of us. We fell in love with our guest whose utter difference from us was beguiling, at times hilarious, but at the end we formed a deeply intimate relation derived from its uniqueness.

We learned about Japan, and he learned about America (and also probably a lot about France and Argentina to boot) and my father was able to take deep knowledge to the corporation that now knew how to approach a heretofore somewhat mysterious culture.

There were times, of course, when we sensed we had inadvertently upset our guest, as he also realized that aspects of his own natural way of being threw us off. We worked our way through these inevitable glitches *in our own way*, by which I mean that we developed our *own shared culture* that derived solely from person-to-person lived experience.

This was a so-called cultural exchange, and for those of you old enough to recall the cold war you will remember how vital it was that the Soviets and the Americans agreed upon exchange of artists, musicians, scientists, and so forth in order to build bridges where otherwise the politics of difference were moving ahead at terrifying and destructive speed.

If the enlightened international community agreed to fund a "cultural gap year" for all postgraduates in different countries, such that post-BA students spent three months at a time, for three periods (hence living in three differing countries) I think this would change the world.

We do not need Richard Branson to find exit strategies for the wealthy and privileged, trying to get us to Mars not only because it is too late for that, but because it is *wrong*. We have to get closer to one another, we have to break bread together, and we have to begin with 21-year-olds who we can easily fund to live in families in 3 countries over a 1-year span *before* they go into the workplace or on to professional or graduate studies.

This segment of my talk has been devoted to what we can think of as "ego integrative" activities that help us deal with the present and the future, the emphasis being on the development of worldliness in order that we inform the impersonal imperatives of globalization with the knowledge derived from the human community.

But we face an important hurdle, which I now address.

26 Id-Capitalism

Capitalism—or market forces if you will—is a much-discussed topic, and I will not review its history or its many meanings. Instead, I will take as an axiom that capitalism is simply a necessarily ruthless (and impersonal) system that follows the forces of supply, demand, and investment. It is to the self, nation, and world what the id is to the ego. To say that we are anti-capitalist would be, then, equivalent to stating we are against the id.

The id and capitalism could be one and the same: ruthless features of human nature that follow the drives of sexuality and aggression (the id) or greed: profit over people, and annihilation of any impediments to the drive that is capitalism.

If someone proposed to me that they had decided they hated their id and were devoted to immunization against it through differing forms of id dispossession (reduction of sexual and aggressive drives, diminishment of greed, avarice, envy, hate, etc.), I would be concerned that at the very least they were neurotic or developing an impossible to survive character. If someone said they hated capitalism and repudiated it, I would think they were in much the same camp as those who were opposed to the id.

If, on the other hand, someone proposed to me that they believed that market forces should be left alone and that such forces were self-correcting, I would think this was equivalent to letting pedophiles govern schools and teach all the children, or sexual predators operate and man sexual abuse clinics. In other words, it would be at best perverse and more worryingly, psychotic.

The id and capitalism are existential features of human nature, and to repudiate them is to wish away parts of ourselves that will not go away, nor should we try to do so. But without the modifying functions of the ego and the superego, the id would wreak havoc around the world and so too with capitalism. Unregulated, allowed to simply move according to the market forces, is to destroy the human race.

In perhaps no other segment of our societies do we see the problems posed to the psyche by capitalism as much as we do in the "business community." It is there—in that commune—that people from all walks of the capitalist world meet and greet and exchange views. It is there that coaches, consultants, and reasoned managers will meet up with a very troubling (if recurrent) factor in social evolution: that is, the rise and normalization of sociopathy.

Whether you know it or not—and obviously I think it is important to know this—those who inhabit graduate business schools are unconsciously delegated the task of developing the dynamics of the ethical (DOTE), which I define here as the task of micro-regulation of id-capitalism through coaching and consultations with individual clients and institutions.

Just as we can change the world through the gap year I discussed moments ago, so too can those who work within the business community change the world if the DOTE is given time and consideration by those of you in consultancy and management.

But what does this entail?

What do you actually do?

Time does not permit a discussion of the challenges of working with (and working through) the new normal of sociopathy, but we need to respect this social evolution rather than condemn it. The sociopathic dimension in all of us is an ego decision to facilitate the movements of id-capitalism while selling the self, the community, the world, on the merits of this development.

The oil and gas industry, for example, spends huge sums of money on Academy Award advertisements selling the public on the benefits to society of oil extraction and processing, knowing that the rise of particulate matter (pm) 2.5 is killing millions of people a year in the large metropolises in the world. The rise of air pollution—the direct outcome not of climate change but of human pollution—has made Los Angeles a health risk to all the inhabitants and those of you from India and Asia do not need to know from me how pm 2.5 is probably the leading single health hazard in the world.

The art of coaching and consulting in some institutions will be to help companies see into the future, to the point where a population will rise up against their productions unless significant changes are made. Revolutionary discontent is now latent around the world and exceedingly dangerous to everyone. And who would have thought that the new leadership would be cultivated right here, at INSEAD, and other business schools around the world while in the past they would have come from seminaries, schools of government, international relations, departments of history, politics, or the wide realm of the humanities. That was true of the nineteenth and twentieth centuries but is not so now.

Globalization is simply human progress as was the development of nuclear weapons. We can mourn the loss of a less dangerous and imperiling universe, or, we can do what we have always done: we can put our minds together (as we have discussed over these last few days), and we can build ethical and intelligent psychologically informed units within the organizational world so that the humane being continues to evolve from the human being, vital to our survival as a species.

Notes

Chapter 1

1 Frantz Fanon. "The Fact of Blackness," in *Theories of Race and Racism*, ed. Les Black and John Solomos (London and New York: Routledge, 2008), 257.

2 Jose Ortega y Gasset. *Man and Crisis* (New York: WW Norton, 1958), 140.

3 William Bradford. *Of Plymouth Plantation 1620–1647* (New York: Modern Library, 1981).

4 Richard Hofstadter. *The Paranoid Style in American Politics* (New York: Vintage, [1952] 2008). See also, David S. Brown. *Richard Hofstadter: An Intellectual Biography* (Chicago and London: The University of Chicago Press, 2006).

5 S. Freud and Andreas-Salome Lou. *Letters*, ed. Ernst Pfeiffer (New York and London: W.W. Norton, 1985).

6 It is fascinating and prescient that both Anna Freud and Heinz Hartman—on the cusp of WWII—while founding ego psychology incorporate war and its impact on the self through metaphor in their theory of the ego. (Japan had already invaded Manchuria in 1931 and was on the verge of invading China. The "atmosphere" of war was present when both authors were writing these seminal texts). AF: "When the relation between two neighboring powers—ego and id—are peaceful" then all is well and "in favorable cases the ego does not object to the intruder" (6) but "peaceful relations between the neighboring powers are at an end" at times and instinctual impulses may launch "a surprise attack. The ego on its side becomes suspicious; it proceeds to counterattack and to invade the territory of the id" (7). HH: "to use an analogy, the description of a country, a nation, a state, includes, besides its involvements in wars with neighboring nations or states, its boundaries and the peacetime traffic across the borders" (11) and writing of "the borderland of the ego" "the effectiveness of the armies defending the borders also depends on the support they get or do not get from the rear" (15). It is telling and moving that in *some* respects their ego psychology is *itself* an effort of the ego to adapt to and survive the horrors

of their era. Both Anna Freud's and Hartmann's works were published within one year of one another. See Anna Freud. *The Ego and the Mechanisms of Defense.* (London: Hogarth, [1936] 1968). Hartmann's work is sited elsewhere in these footnotes. The finest psychoanalytical study of war is Franco Fornari's (1966) *The Psychoanalysis of War* (Bloomington and London: Indiana University Press, 1975). For a brilliant essay on the influence of the events of the Second World War on Freud's theories, see "Freud's study of Moses as a daydream: a biographical essay," in Ilse Grubrich-Simitis, *Early Freud and Late Freud: Reading Anew Studies On Hysteria and Moses and Monotheism* (London: Routledge, 1997), 53–89.

7 Freud, S. 1915 "Thoughts for the Times on War and Death," in *Standard Edition of the Complete Works of Sigmund Freud*, vol. XIV (New York: Hogarth, 1915), 273–300.

8 In (2000) *The Modern Mind: An Intellectual History of the Twentieth Century* (New York: Perennial, 2002) Peter Watson—who writes perhaps the best single volume on western thought since the beginning of the twenty-first century, embraces western science as the single most redeeming accomplishment of the twentieth century. One can of course also include remarkable evolutions in art, music, fiction, and so forth. The point is not that the world stopped progressing, it is that *on balance* the weighty figure of human greed, destructiveness, and indifference marginalizes human creativity.

9 Active destruction is not difficult to identify, such as in a genocide. The more pervasive form of human destructiveness, however, is passive destruction. This is when selves, groups, or nations remain inactive when intervention would halt a destructive process.

10 cited in Salmi Hannu. *Nineteenth Century Europe* (Cambridge: Polity, 2008).

11 See David A. Ross. *Critical Companion to W.B. Yeats: A Literary Reference to His Life and Work* (New York: Infobase, 2009), 220 (available online).

12 Who could have foreseen the "bloodless" murder only twenty-five years later—the Holocaust—the first industrialization of murder? It was beyond imagination.

13 For Heinz Hartmann, adaptation always takes account of the future. "A State of Adaptation May Refer to the Present and to the Future. The Process of Adaptation Always Implies Reference to a Future Condition," in *Ego Psychology and the Problem of Adaptation*, First delivered in 1937, first published 1938 (New York: International Universities Press, 1958), 24.

14 Frantz Fanon. *Black Skin, White Masks* (New York: Grove, [1952] 2008).

15 By this I mean that as we are overwhelmed by the sheer number of seemingly unsolvable problems the inclination to not see them—to induce a protective social blindness—is a clear temptation.

16 Masud Khan's concept of "cumulative trauma" might serve us well as a theoretical construct to identify the imbrication of oppression in the modern self. See Masud Khan, "The Concept of Cumulative Trauma," in *The Privacy of the Self* (London: Hogarth, [1963] 1974), 42–58.

17 Stampp, Kenneth M. *The Peculiar Institution: Slavery in the Antebellum South* (New York: Vintage, 1956).

18 There are several psychoanalytical essays on pseudo stupidity. I think that Margaret Mahler's essay on pseudoimbecility is a masterpiece. See "Pseudoimbecility: A Magic Cap of Invisibility," in Margaret S. Mahler, *The Selected Papers of Margaret S. Mahler. Volume One: Infantile Psychosis and Early Contributions* (New York, Jason Aronson, [1942] 1979), 3–16.

19 See Frantz Fanon. *Black Skin, White Masks* (New York: Grove, [1952] 2008), 95.

20 For a psychoanalytical study of "mental slavery," see Barbara Fletchman. Smith *Mental Slavery: Psychoanalytical Studies of Caribbean People* (London: Rebus Press, 2000). Also see Nancy Hollander. *Uprooted Minds: Surviving the Politics of Terror in the Americas* (New York & London: Routledge, 2010). Hollander's book is a fine study of many of the factors that now contribute to wide spread mental pain in large parts of our world.

21 I address the transformation from mourning to melancholia resident in Western populations from the mid-twentieth century to the early twenty-first century in *Meaning and Melancholia* (in preparation, publication in 2016).

22 It is "psychically systemic" when selves turn to the internet without thinking, using it for hours a day, so that it is now part of the fabric of one's being.

23 See Danah Boyd. *Its Complicated. The Social Life of Networked Teens* (New Haven: Yale, 2014). This book is an invaluable resource in understanding the many myths about contemporary youths' use of the social network.

24 For a discussion of that psychic nourishment derived from the self's encounter with evocative objects and the concept of the receptive unconscious, please see Christopher Bollas. *Being a Character* (London: Routledge, 1992) and *The Evocative Object World* (London, Routledge, 2009).

25 Bollas, Christopher. "The Transmisive Self and Transmissive Objects," in *Fear and Fantasy in a Global World* (Rodopi Press, in preparation).

26 Don DeLillo. *Cosmopolis* (New York: Scribner, 2003).

27 Simon Head. *Mindless: Why Smarter Machines are Making Dumber Humans* (New York: Basic Books, 2014).

28 A neologism intended to signify the fusion of speed, the internet, and social networking.

29 The clinical samples in this essay are derived from Anglo-American analysands. Psychoanalysts from other cultures may, therefore, be somewhat puzzled by these examples and, if so may wish to substitute new forms of expression emerging in their own cultures, if that is so.

30 "Action thought" is an important idea of Heinz Kohut's that bears on my use of the term operationalism. See Heinz Kohut. *The Restoration of the Self* (New York: International Universities Press, 1977), 36–48. Also see "the organizing personality" by Lawrence Hedges in Lawrence Hedges. *Listening Perspectives in Psychotherapy* (Northvale: Jason Aronson, 1983), 225–64.

31 The clinical samples reflect segments of North American culture and will not typify idioms of expression found in many other cultures and countries. However, as globalization began as a largely US movement, and, as many countries around the world have adapted US idioms—vestimentary, alimentary, linguistic, etc.—it may benefit psychoanalysis if one puts aside ones own incredulity (i.e.,"this cannot happen *here*") as globalization—if truly effective—will "Americanize" the world.

32 For an interesting discussion of the limit of horizontal thinking, please see George S. Klein. *Perception, Motives, and Personality* (New York: Alfred Knopf, 1970), 130–1.

33 There is a considerable literature on the concept of "the spectacle," beginning with the work of Guy Debord and the "situationists" of the mid-twentieth century.

34 For an invaluable exploration of the role of insight in psychoanalysis, please see R. Horacio Etchegoyen. *The Fundamentals of Psychoanalytic Technique* (London: Karnac, 1991), 653–88.

35 Of course, the analysand's quizzical response is not a resistance but an unconscious request for further analysis. So, although he is refractive, horizontalizing, and operationalizing, he is also unconsciously receptive to the anlayst's comment.

36 Jameson's critique of contemporary culture in *Postmodernism: Or the Cultural Logic of Late Capitalism* (Durham, Duke University Press, 1991) is the benchmark for all cultural studies of the late twentieth century. While I disagree with much of his argument—and his idiosyncratic formulations of psychoanalytical theory—his work is brilliant and intellectually inspiring. There are too many works to cite that comment on the death of the subject, but a crucial late twentieth century text is Alain Badiou. *Theory of the Subject* (London and New York: Continuum, 1982) and the foremost psychoanalytical cultural critique of the twenty-first century surely is Slavoj Zizek and his *Living in the End Times* (London, New York: Verso, 2010) is essential reading.

37 See John Steiner. *Psychic Retreats* (London: Routledge, 1993).

38 In philosophy, there are as many definitions of the "subject" as there are philosophers. I use the term with some hesitation but in accord, I think, with the Freudian theory of the unconscious as the seat of human perception, organization, agency, and communication.

39 I have since discovered that Frantz Fanon used this term--"objecthood"--to describe the state of being of the oppressed self. See "The Fact of blackness" above. Also see Christopher Bollas. "Being an Object, Being an Other," in *Dark at the End of the Tunnel* (London: Free Association Books, 2004), 39–62.

40 See Christopher Bollas. "The Normotic," in *The Shadow of the Object* (London: Free Association Books, 1987). See Joyce McDougall. *Theatres of the Body* (New York: WW Norton, 1989) for her discussion of "normopaths."

41 See for example, P. Fonagy and M. Target (1998) "Mentalization and the Changing Aims of Child Psychoanalysis," *Psychoanalytic Dialogues* 8 (1998): 87–114.

42 I do not take the view that capitalism is somehow to blame for the ills of mankind. It is simply an economic system inherently amoral—it would be defeated by any moral imperatives—and even if regulated, it nonetheless can only thrive if profit is put before people. Nor should capitalism be confused with "private enterprise" or the work of the "entrepreneur" neither of which are inevitably dependent upon capitalism.

43 Freud imagined the life and death instincts as intrapsychic forces, but if we understand the death instinct as a critical factor in global capitalism (in which the human dimension has withdrawn into the narcissism of the singular life and into the illusions of the good life) and in psychotic group processes (as in terrorist movements or genocidal outbreaks) then the attentions of psychoanalysis should take into account this "outbreak" of the death drive and its bearing on contemporary civilization.

44 As of this writing, the United Nations has announced plans to construct "weather reports from the future" using well-known weather reporters in countries around the world to try to wake up the public to the alarming situation now threatening the planet. See "United Nations Predicts Climate Hell in 2050 with Imagined Weather Forecasts," *The Guardian*, September 1, 2014, 14.18 EDT.

45 Obviously, fundamentalists of whatever religious order would claim to have very high ideals indeed. In that respect, however, there is a noteworthy increased divide not simply between believers and non-believers, but also between so-called religious moderates and the fundamentalists.

46 One of the great losses has been our belief in the function of history. Without it, left in the malignantly disseminative effect of refractive thought, we are unable to *contextualize* shocking events, and the ego is thus disabled from forming a generatively adaptive strategy. As of this writing, ISIS (ISIL) is terrifying the West and reported by US defense decretary Chuck Hagel as "beyond anything we have seen"--or Obama as "a cancer," spreading throughout the world.

Beyond anything we have seen? Really? Or just not seen if we eradicate world history?

Unable to think about the "unseen"—other than how do we kill it?—we have abandoned the work of history even to the point of not realizing that this relatively small band of Sunni militants would not have rampaged across Syria and Iraq were it not for the failures of democracy after the Arab Spring, were it not for the elimination by Egypt of the moderate influence of the Muslim Brotherhood, and were it not for Al-Maliki's elimination of the Sunni's from participation in Iraq government. In other words, ISIS makes sense if we *think* about them rather than simply refract them. We *have* seen the likes of ISIS for thousands of years.

47 Perhaps for obvious reasons, the West prefers to focus on Islamic fundamentalism as a threat to a diverse and tolerant world. This ignores the malignant reality of fundamentalism in all monotheistic orders, and that certainly includes modern Christian and Jewish fundamentalism that ordains their own forms of intellectual genocide. But fundamentalism exists in non-religious movements and has as much to do with the ordinary "fascist state of mind" to be found in ordinary "intellectual genocide." Please see Christopher Bollas. "The Fascist State of Mind," in *Being a Character* (London: Routledge, 1992).

48 Hartman's concept of adaptation is highly sophisticated, and he carefully defines the interactive role between social psychology and the individual. "The social structure determines, at least in part, the adaptive chances of a particular form of behavior, by the term *social compliance*. . . . Social compliance is a special form of the environmental 'compliance' which is implied by the concept of adaptation" (31). See *Ego Psychology and the Problem of Adaptation*, presented in 1937, published in 1939 (New York: International Universities Press, 1958).

49 Christopher Lasch provided the first extensive psychoanalytical study of the movement toward a diminishment of higher-level mental functioning in order to deal with the increasing impoverishments of human possibility in the late twentieth century. His visionary work is acutely relevant to analysis of the early twenty-first century and the crisis in thinking. See Christopher Lasch. *The Minimal Self: Psychic Survival in Troubled Times* (New York: WW Norton, 1984).

50 For over thirty years, there has been a fading of interest in the humanities. The canary in the coal mine may be the movement in the United States to eliminate departments of English literature. See "Pulling the Plug on English Departments" by David Masciotra in *The Daily Beast*, July 28, 2014 (5.45 a.m. EST).

51 J.-B. Pontalis. *Frontiers in Psychoanalysis: Between the Dream and Psychic Pain* (London: Hogarth, [1977] 1981), 191.

52 In *this* respect, one may identify the manic reach of the work of Hegel. And *afterward* one sees the depressive depths of Kirkegaard. If Neitsche oscillates between the manic and the depressive one notes that Husserl, Heidegger, Sartre, and laterly Badiou seek thought-universes in which the mind-self can take refuge from the shock of the real. Of course, intense conflict elicits works of genius and in that respect there is some consolation for the harried pace of modern life.

Chapter 2

1 Virginia Woolf. *A Writer's Diary* (San Diego, New York, London: Harcourt, Inc, 1982), 55.

2 For a discussion of "psychic genera" please see Christopher Bollas. *Being A Character* (London: Routledge, 1992) and *the Evocative Object World* (New York: Routledge, 2009).

3 E. M. Forster. *Howards End* (Cassia Press, 2009).

4 "We learn . . . that an unconscious idea is as such quite incapable of entering the preconscious and that it can only exercise any effect thereby establishing a connection with an idea which already belongs to the preconscious, by transferring its intensity on to it and by getting itself 'covered' by it. Here we have the fact of 'transference', which provides an explanation of so many striking phenomena in the mental life of neurotics. The preconscious idea, which thus acquires an undeserved degree of intensity, may either be left unaltered by the transference, or it may have a modification forced upon it, derived from the content of the idea which effects the transference." S. Freud. *The Interpretation of Dreams* (1900), 562–3.

Chapter 23

1 See Jonah Lehrer. "The Virtues of Daydreaming," *The New Yorker*, June 5, 2012.

www.ingramcontent.com/pod-product-compliance
Ingram Content Group UK Ltd.
Pitfield, Milton Keynes, MK11 3LW, UK
UKHW021849130926
475466UK00003B/40

9 798216 202035